W. VANCE - J. VAN HAMME

THE DAY OF THE BLACK SUN

XIII

Colour work: PETRA

9th CINEBOOK
The 9th Art Publisher

Original title: Le jour du soleil noir

Original edition: © Dargaud Benelux (Dargaud-Lombard SA), 1984
by Van Hamme, Vance & Petra
www.dargaud.com
All rights reserved

Lettering and text layout: Imadjinn
Printed in Spain by Just Colour Graphic

This edition first published in Great Britain in 2010 by
Cinebook Ltd
56 Beech Avenue
Canterbury, Kent
CT4 7TA
www.cinebook.com

A CIP catalogue record for this book
is available from the British Library

ISBN 978-1-84918-039-9

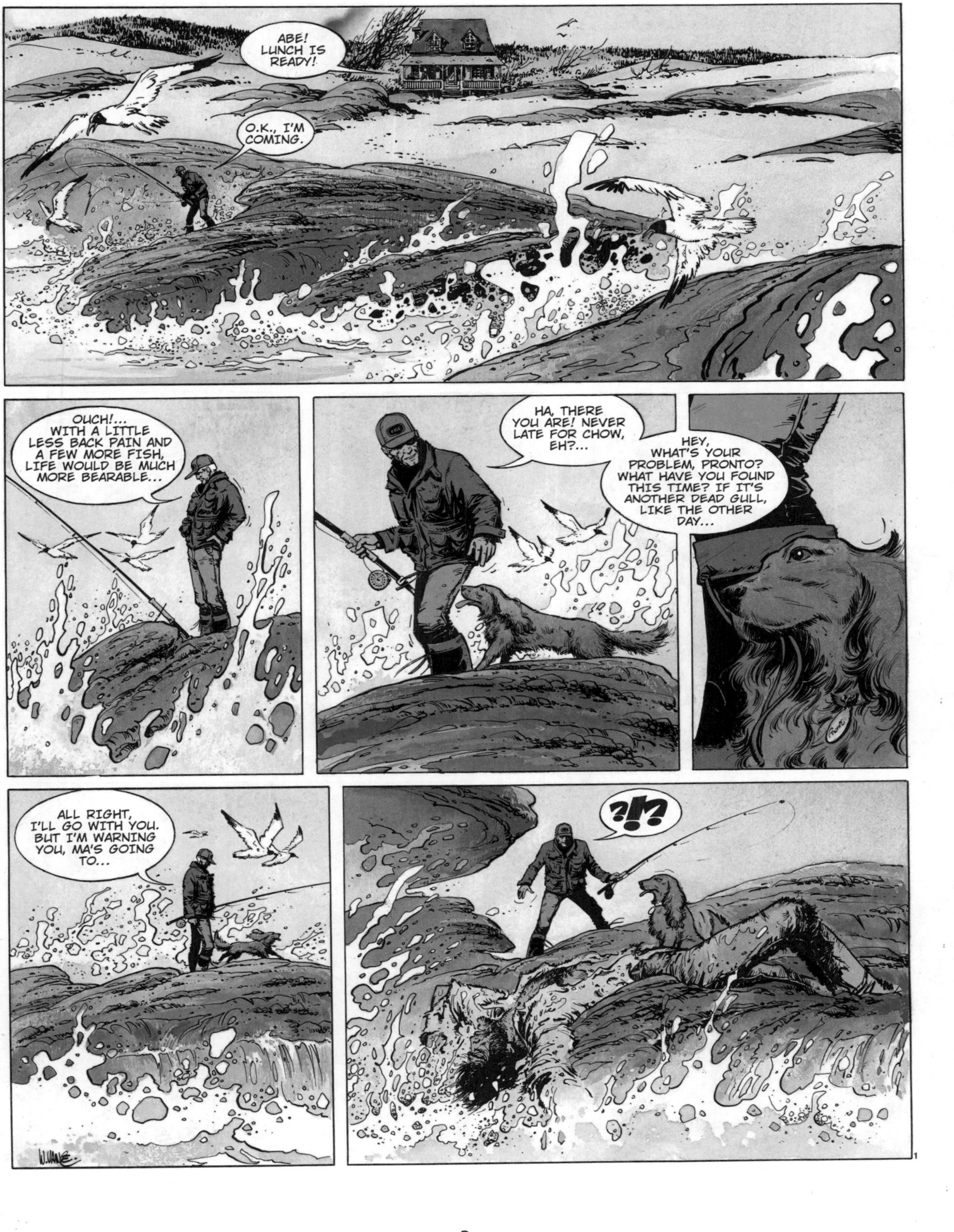
ABE! LUNCH IS READY!
O.K., I'M COMING.
OUCH!... WITH A LITTLE LESS BACK PAIN AND A FEW MORE FISH, LIFE WOULD BE MUCH MORE BEARABLE...
HA, THERE YOU ARE! NEVER LATE FOR CHOW, EH?...
HEY, WHAT'S YOUR PROBLEM, PRONTO? WHAT HAVE YOU FOUND THIS TIME? IF IT'S ANOTHER DEAD GULL, LIKE THE OTHER DAY...
ALL RIGHT, I'LL GO WITH YOU. BUT I'M WARNING YOU, MA'S GOING TO...
?!!

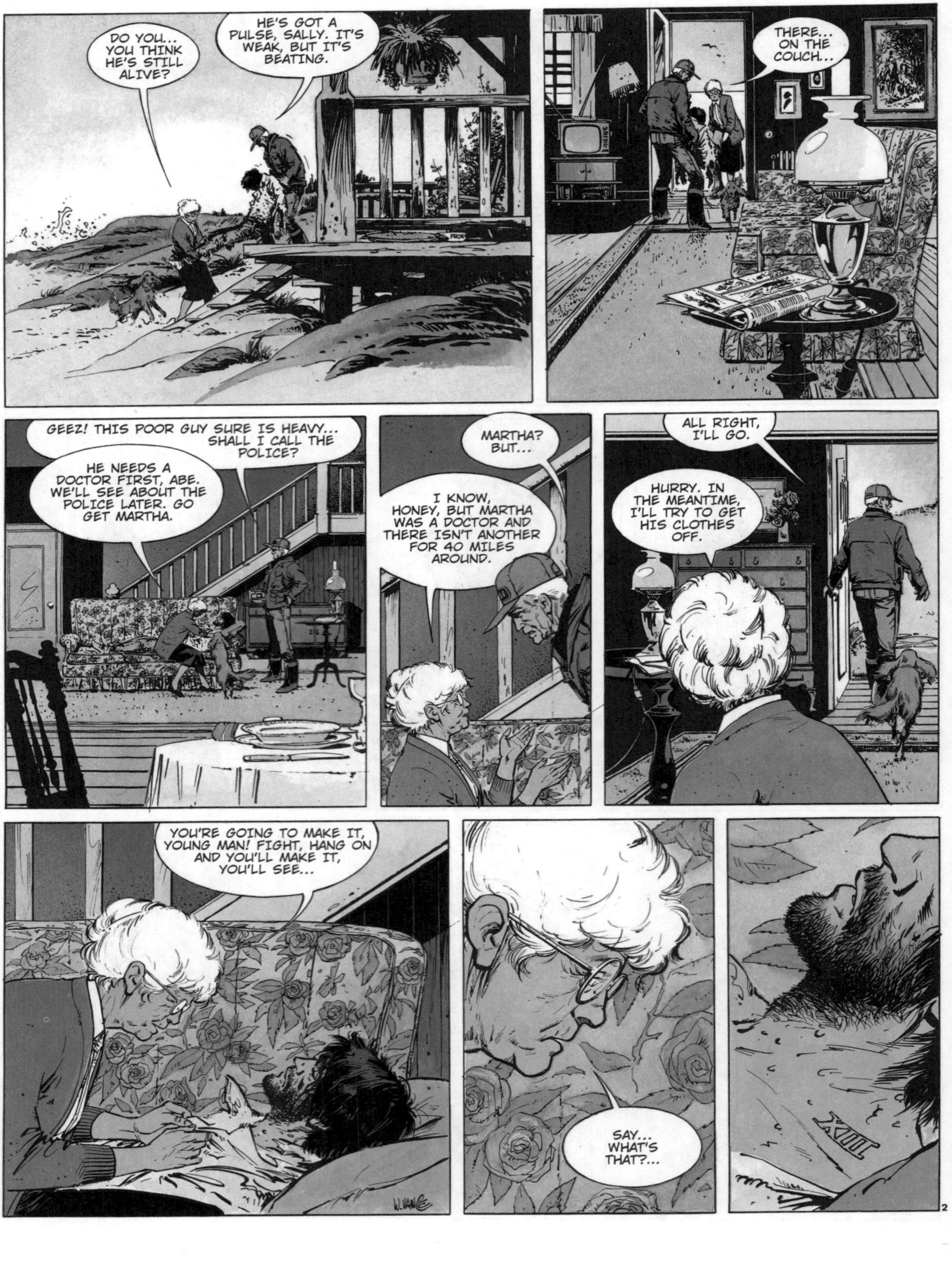

DO YOU... YOU THINK HE'S STILL ALIVE?
HE'S GOT A PULSE, SALLY. IT'S WEAK, BUT IT'S BEATING.
THERE... ON THE COUCH...
GEEZ! THIS POOR GUY SURE IS HEAVY... SHALL I CALL THE POLICE?
HE NEEDS A DOCTOR FIRST, ABE. WE'LL SEE ABOUT THE POLICE LATER. GO GET MARTHA.
MARTHA? BUT...
I KNOW, HONEY, BUT MARTHA WAS A DOCTOR AND THERE ISN'T ANOTHER FOR 40 MILES AROUND.
ALL RIGHT, I'LL GO.
HURRY. IN THE MEANTIME, I'LL TRY TO GET HIS CLOTHES OFF.
YOU'RE GOING TO MAKE IT, YOUNG MAN! FIGHT, HANG ON AND YOU'LL MAKE IT, YOU'LL SEE...
SAY... WHAT'S THAT?...
XIII
2

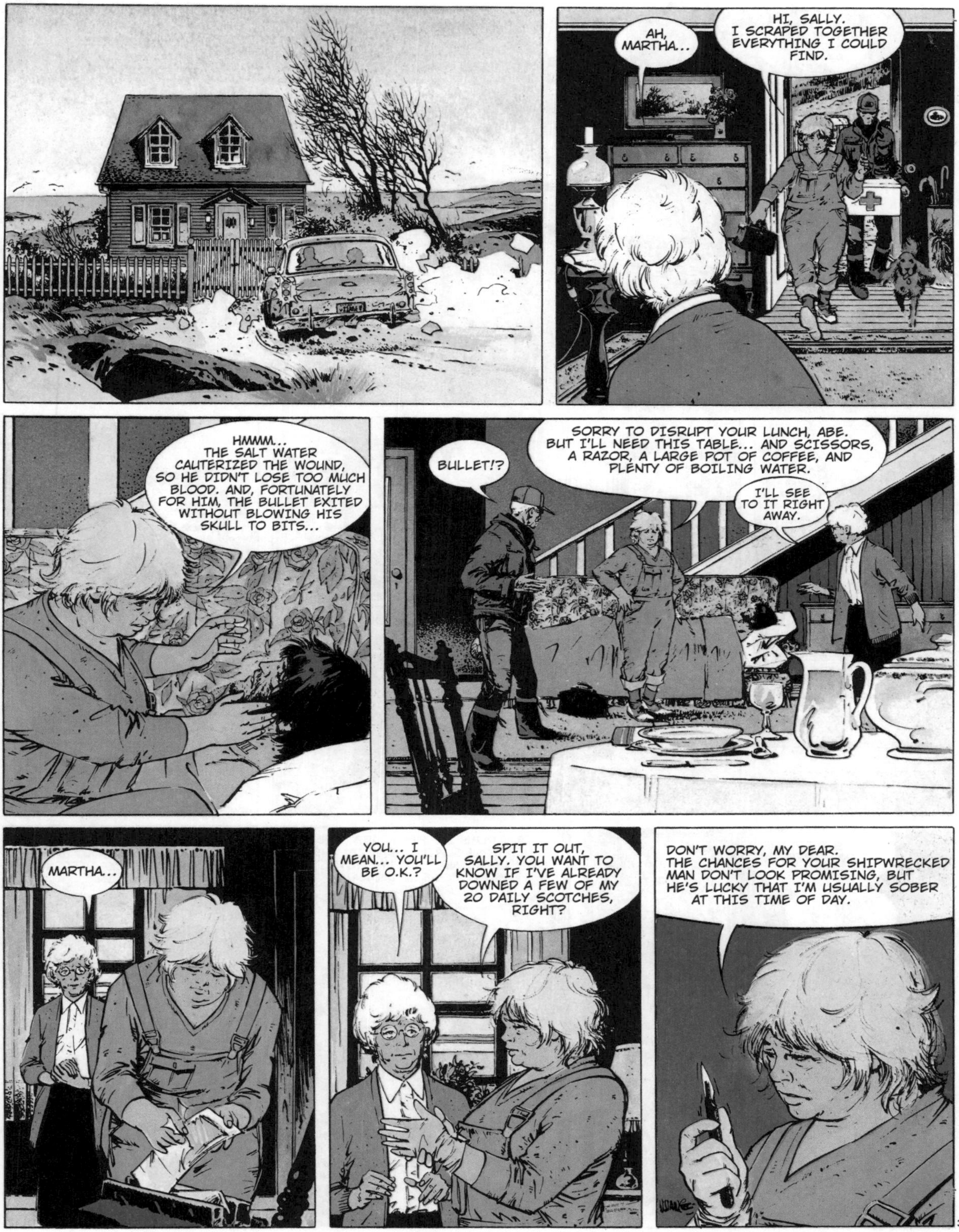
AH, MARTHA...
HI, SALLY. I SCRAPED TOGETHER EVERYTHING I COULD FIND.
HMMM... THE SALT WATER CAUTERIZED THE WOUND, SO HE DIDN'T LOSE TOO MUCH BLOOD. AND, FORTUNATELY FOR HIM, THE BULLET EXITED WITHOUT BLOWING HIS SKULL TO BITS...
BULLET!?
SORRY TO DISRUPT YOUR LUNCH, ABE. BUT I'LL NEED THIS TABLE... AND SCISSORS, A RAZOR, A LARGE POT OF COFFEE, AND PLENTY OF BOILING WATER.
I'LL SEE TO IT RIGHT AWAY.
MARTHA...
YOU... I MEAN... YOU'LL BE O.K.?
SPIT IT OUT, SALLY. YOU WANT TO KNOW IF I'VE ALREADY DOWNED A FEW OF MY 20 DAILY SCOTCHES, RIGHT?
DON'T WORRY, MY DEAR. THE CHANCES FOR YOUR SHIPWRECKED MAN DON'T LOOK PROMISING, BUT HE'S LUCKY THAT I'M USUALLY SOBER AT THIS TIME OF DAY.

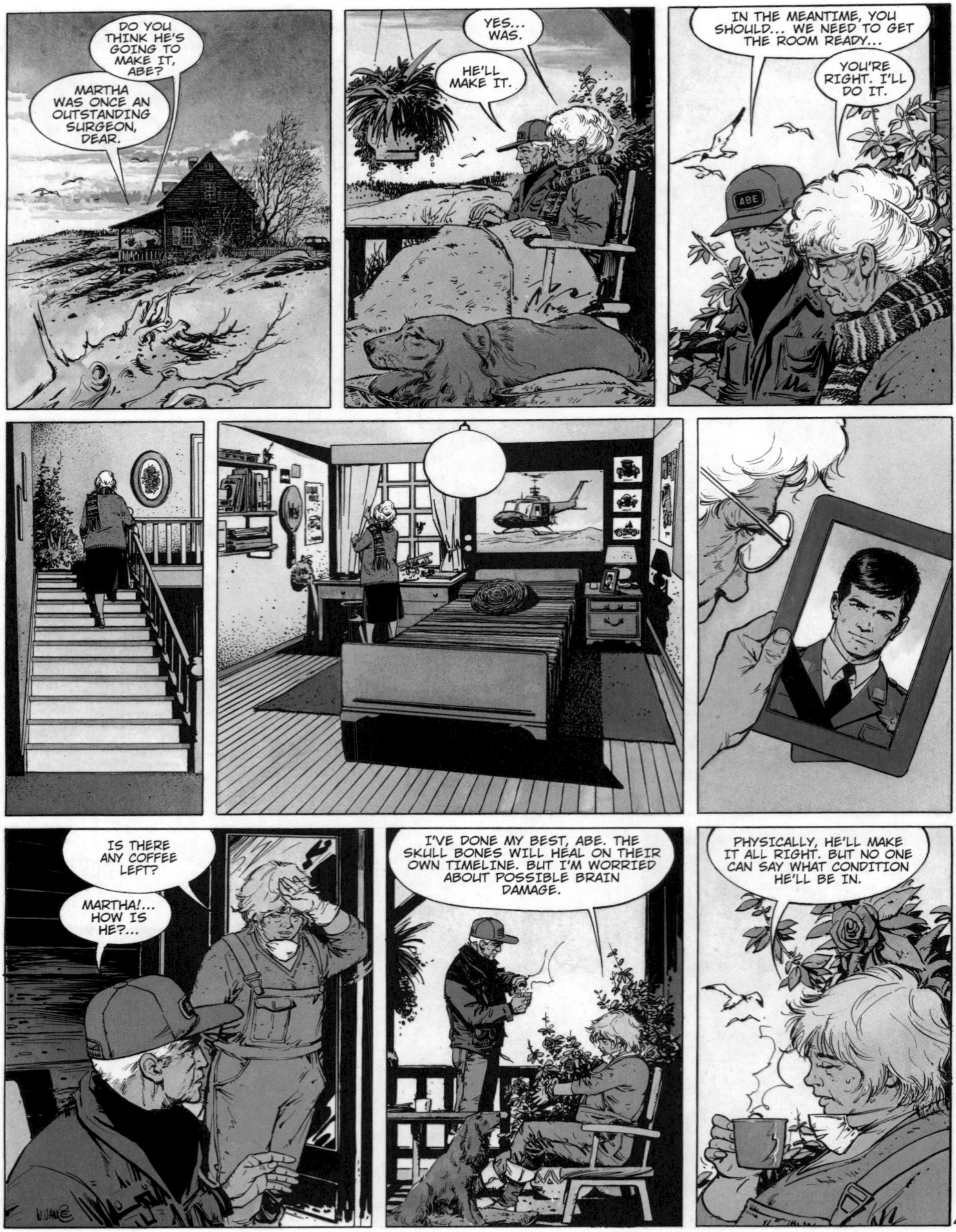
DO YOU THINK HE'S GOING TO MAKE IT, ABE?
MARTHA WAS ONCE AN OUTSTANDING SURGEON, DEAR.
HE'LL MAKE IT.
YES... WAS.
IN THE MEANTIME, YOU SHOULD... WE NEED TO GET THE ROOM READY...
YOU'RE RIGHT. I'LL DO IT.
ABE
IS THERE ANY COFFEE LEFT?
MARTHA!... HOW IS HE?...
I'VE DONE MY BEST, ABE. THE SKULL BONES WILL HEAL ON THEIR OWN TIMELINE. BUT I'M WORRIED ABOUT POSSIBLE BRAIN DAMAGE.
PHYSICALLY, HE'LL MAKE IT ALL RIGHT. BUT NO ONE CAN SAY WHAT CONDITION HE'LL BE IN.
4

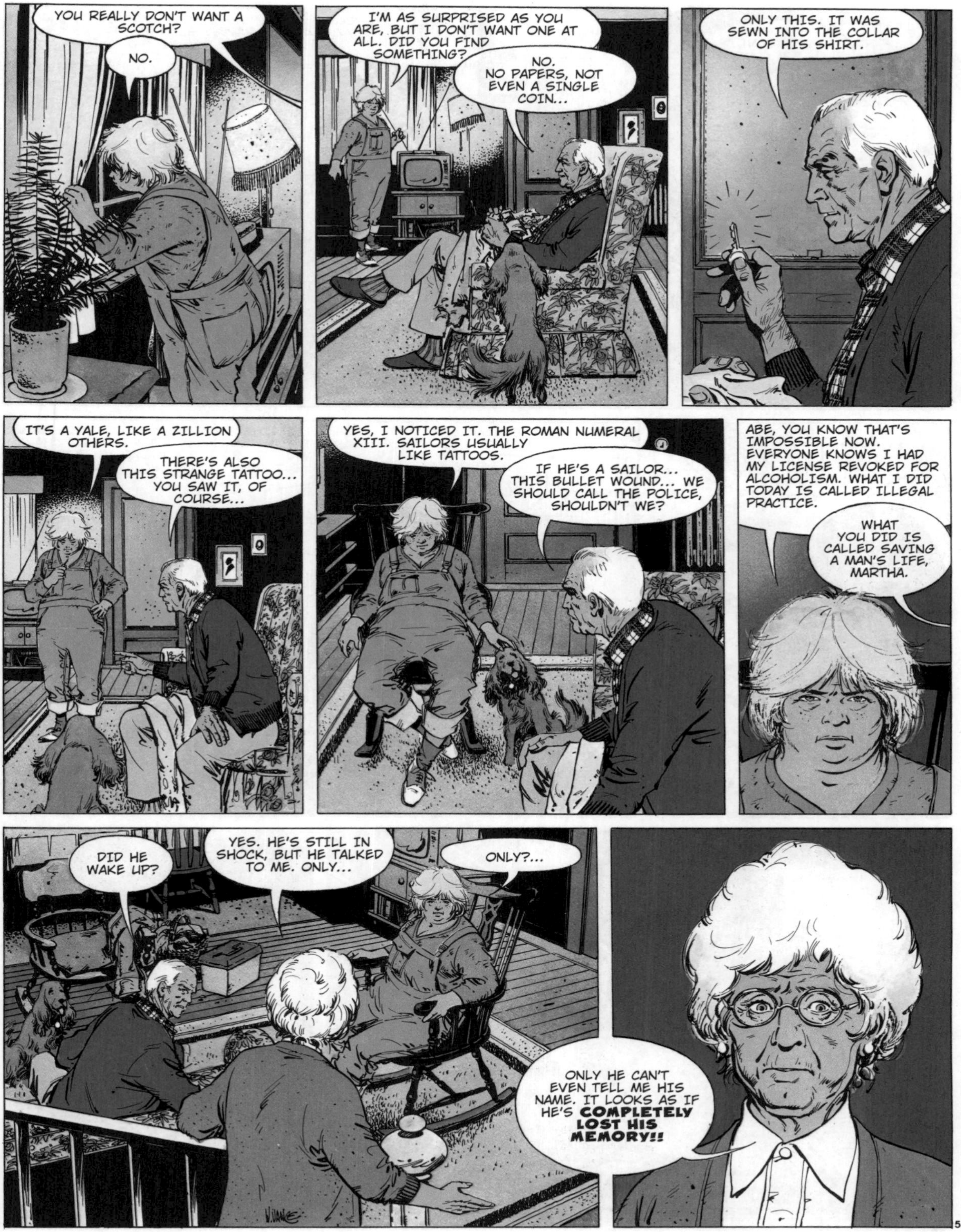
YOU REALLY DON'T WANT A SCOTCH?
NO.
I'M AS SURPRISED AS YOU ARE, BUT I DON'T WANT ONE AT ALL. DID YOU FIND SOMETHING?
NO. NO PAPERS, NOT EVEN A SINGLE COIN...
ONLY THIS. IT WAS SEWN INTO THE COLLAR OF HIS SHIRT.
IT'S A YALE, LIKE A ZILLION OTHERS.
THERE'S ALSO THIS STRANGE TATTOO... YOU SAW IT, OF COURSE...
YES, I NOTICED IT. THE ROMAN NUMERAL XIII. SAILORS USUALLY LIKE TATTOOS.
IF HE'S A SAILOR... THIS BULLET WOUND... WE SHOULD CALL THE POLICE, SHOULDN'T WE?
ABE, YOU KNOW THAT'S IMPOSSIBLE NOW. EVERYONE KNOWS I HAD MY LICENSE REVOKED FOR ALCOHOLISM. WHAT I DID TODAY IS CALLED ILLEGAL PRACTICE.
WHAT YOU DID IS CALLED SAVING A MAN'S LIFE, MARTHA.
DID HE WAKE UP?
YES. HE'S STILL IN SHOCK, BUT HE TALKED TO ME. ONLY...
ONLY?...
ONLY HE CAN'T EVEN TELL ME HIS NAME. IT LOOKS AS IF HE'S **COMPLETELY LOST HIS MEMORY!!**
W. VANCE
5

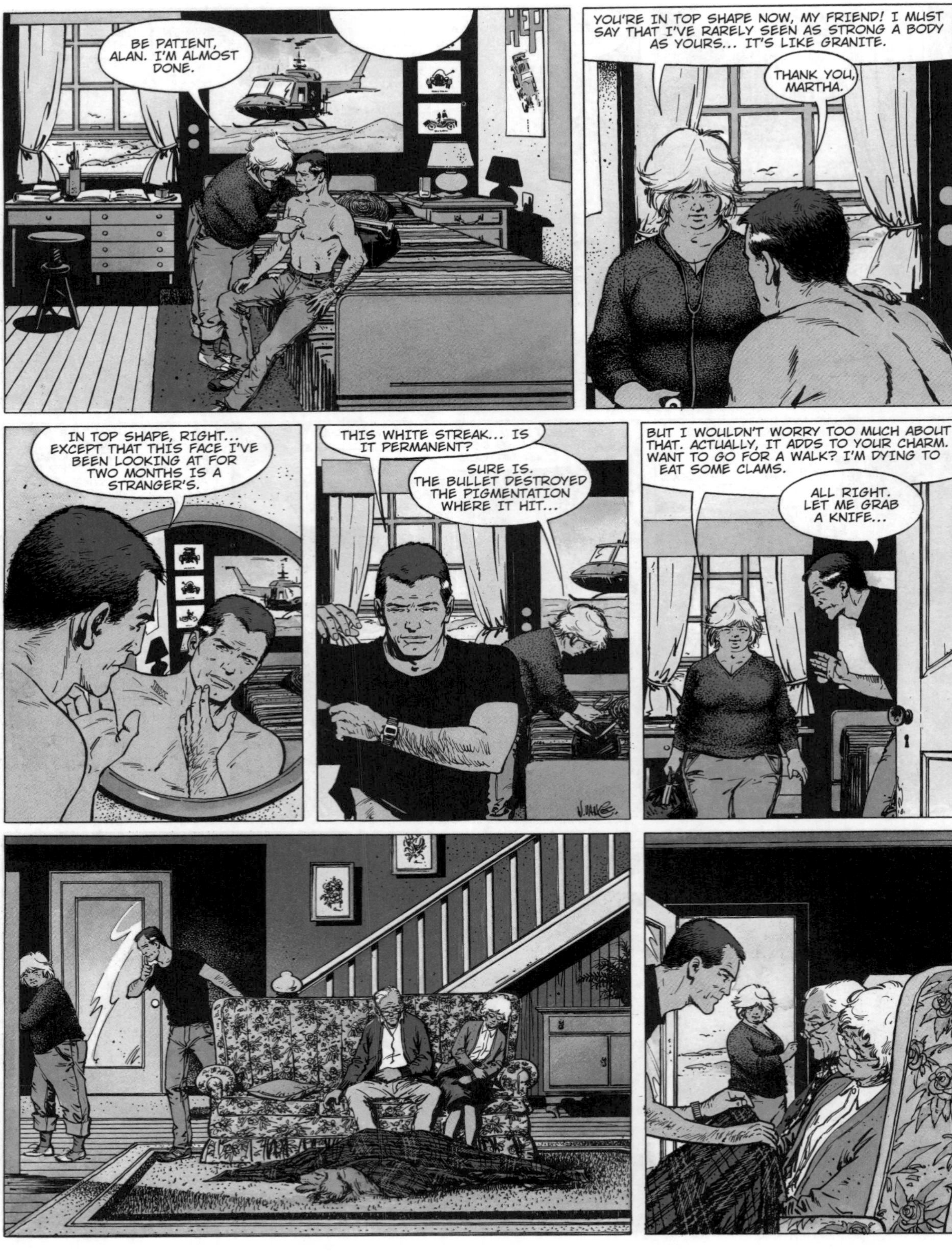

BE PATIENT, ALAN. I'M ALMOST DONE.
YOU'RE IN TOP SHAPE NOW, MY FRIEND! I MUST SAY THAT I'VE RARELY SEEN AS STRONG A BODY AS YOURS... IT'S LIKE GRANITE.
THANK YOU, MARTHA.
IN TOP SHAPE, RIGHT... EXCEPT THAT THIS FACE I'VE BEEN LOOKING AT FOR TWO MONTHS IS A STRANGER'S.
THIS WHITE STREAK... IS IT PERMANENT?
SURE IS. THE BULLET DESTROYED THE PIGMENTATION WHERE IT HIT...
BUT I WOULDN'T WORRY TOO MUCH ABOUT THAT. ACTUALLY, IT ADDS TO YOUR CHARM. WANT TO GO FOR A WALK? I'M DYING TO EAT SOME CLAMS.
ALL RIGHT. LET ME GRAB A KNIFE...
6

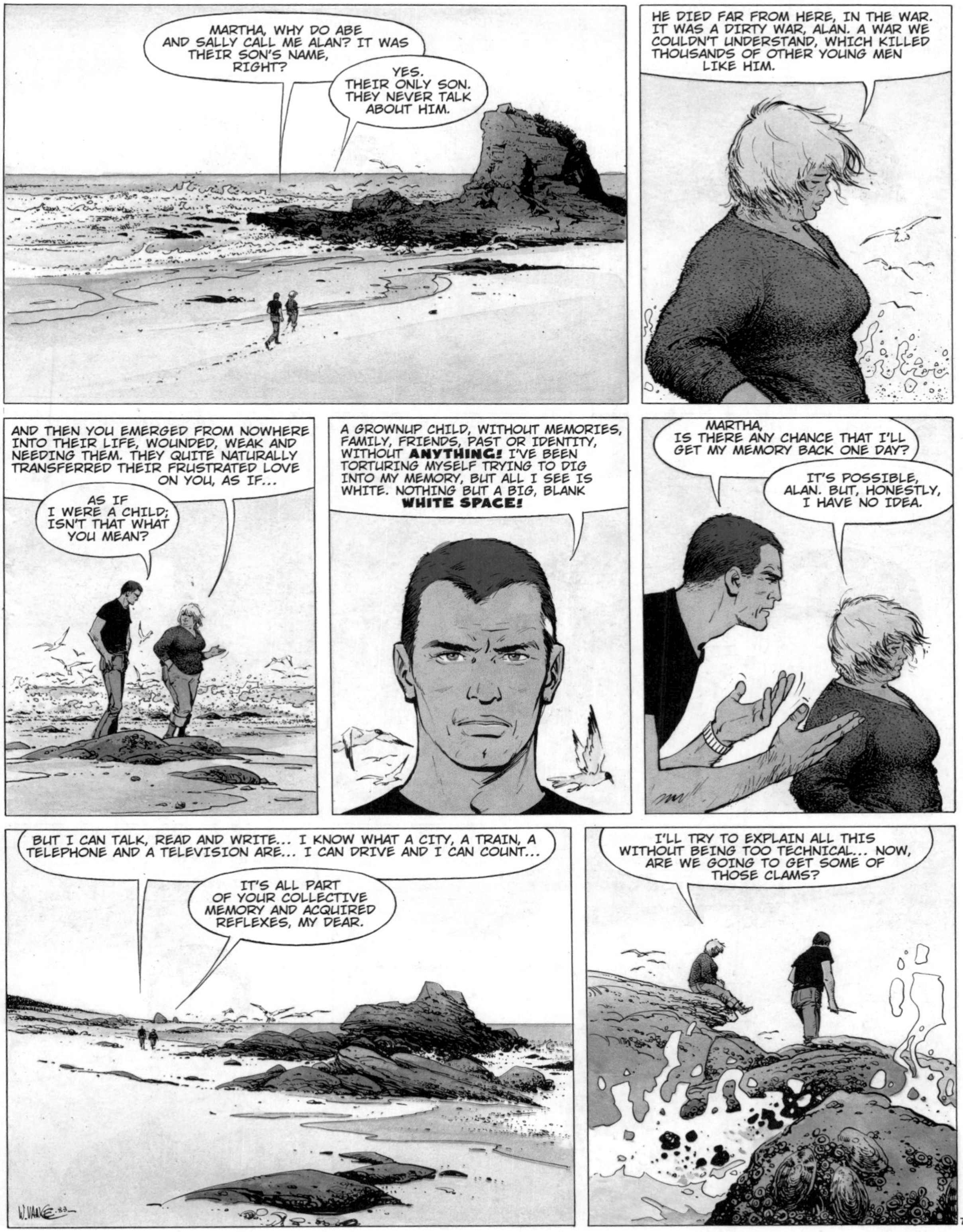
MARTHA, WHY DO ABE AND SALLY CALL ME ALAN? IT WAS THEIR SON'S NAME, RIGHT?
YES. THEIR ONLY SON. THEY NEVER TALK ABOUT HIM.
HE DIED FAR FROM HERE, IN THE WAR. IT WAS A DIRTY WAR, ALAN. A WAR WE COULDN'T UNDERSTAND, WHICH KILLED THOUSANDS OF OTHER YOUNG MEN LIKE HIM.
AND THEN YOU EMERGED FROM NOWHERE INTO THEIR LIFE, WOUNDED, WEAK AND NEEDING THEM. THEY QUITE NATURALLY TRANSFERRED THEIR FRUSTRATED LOVE ON YOU, AS IF...
AS IF I WERE A CHILD; ISN'T THAT WHAT YOU MEAN?
A GROWNUP CHILD, WITHOUT MEMORIES, FAMILY, FRIENDS, PAST OR IDENTITY, WITHOUT **ANYTHING!** I'VE BEEN TORTURING MYSELF TRYING TO DIG INTO MY MEMORY, BUT ALL I SEE IS WHITE. NOTHING BUT A BIG, BLANK **WHITE SPACE!**
MARTHA, IS THERE ANY CHANCE THAT I'LL GET MY MEMORY BACK ONE DAY?
IT'S POSSIBLE, ALAN. BUT, HONESTLY, I HAVE NO IDEA.
BUT I CAN TALK, READ AND WRITE... I KNOW WHAT A CITY, A TRAIN, A TELEPHONE AND A TELEVISION ARE... I CAN DRIVE AND I CAN COUNT...
IT'S ALL PART OF YOUR COLLECTIVE MEMORY AND ACQUIRED REFLEXES, MY DEAR.
I'LL TRY TO EXPLAIN ALL THIS WITHOUT BEING TOO TECHNICAL... NOW, ARE WE GOING TO GET SOME OF THOSE CLAMS?
7

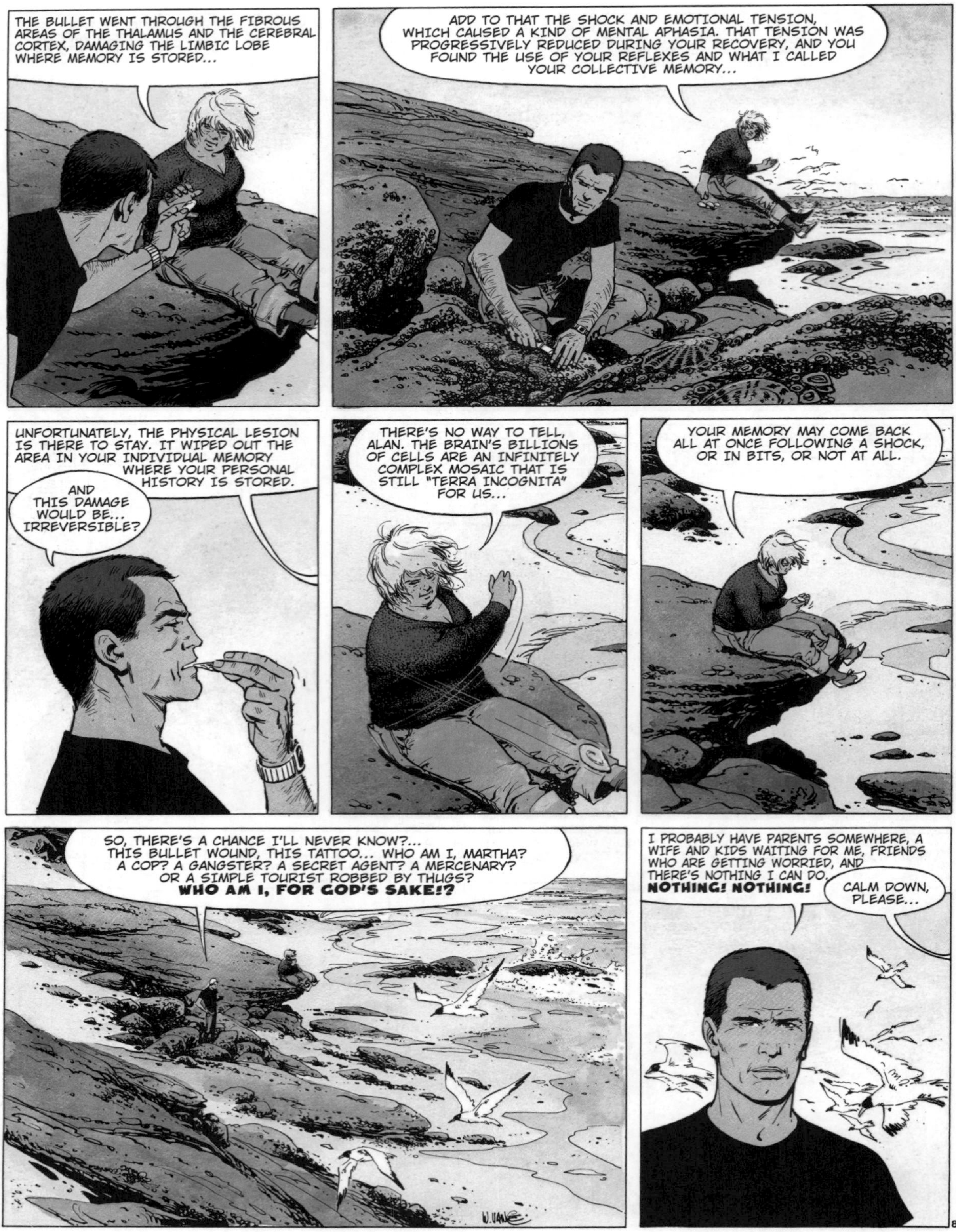
THE BULLET WENT THROUGH THE FIBROUS AREAS OF THE THALAMUS AND THE CEREBRAL CORTEX, DAMAGING THE LIMBIC LOBE WHERE MEMORY IS STORED...
ADD TO THAT THE SHOCK AND EMOTIONAL TENSION, WHICH CAUSED A KIND OF MENTAL APHASIA. THAT TENSION WAS PROGRESSIVELY REDUCED DURING YOUR RECOVERY, AND YOU FOUND THE USE OF YOUR REFLEXES AND WHAT I CALLED YOUR COLLECTIVE MEMORY...
UNFORTUNATELY, THE PHYSICAL LESION IS THERE TO STAY. IT WIPED OUT THE AREA IN YOUR INDIVIDUAL MEMORY WHERE YOUR PERSONAL HISTORY IS STORED.
AND THIS DAMAGE WOULD BE... IRREVERSIBLE?
THERE'S NO WAY TO TELL, ALAN. THE BRAIN'S BILLIONS OF CELLS ARE AN INFINITELY COMPLEX MOSAIC THAT IS STILL "TERRA INCOGNITA" FOR US...
YOUR MEMORY MAY COME BACK ALL AT ONCE FOLLOWING A SHOCK, OR IN BITS, OR NOT AT ALL.
SO, THERE'S A CHANCE I'LL NEVER KNOW?... THIS BULLET WOUND, THIS TATTOO... WHO AM I, MARTHA? A COP? A GANGSTER? A SECRET AGENT? A MERCENARY? OR A SIMPLE TOURIST ROBBED BY THUGS? WHO AM I, FOR GOD'S SAKE!?
W. VANCE
I PROBABLY HAVE PARENTS SOMEWHERE, A WIFE AND KIDS WAITING FOR ME, FRIENDS WHO ARE GETTING WORRIED, AND THERE'S NOTHING I CAN DO. NOTHING! NOTHING!
CALM DOWN, PLEASE...
8

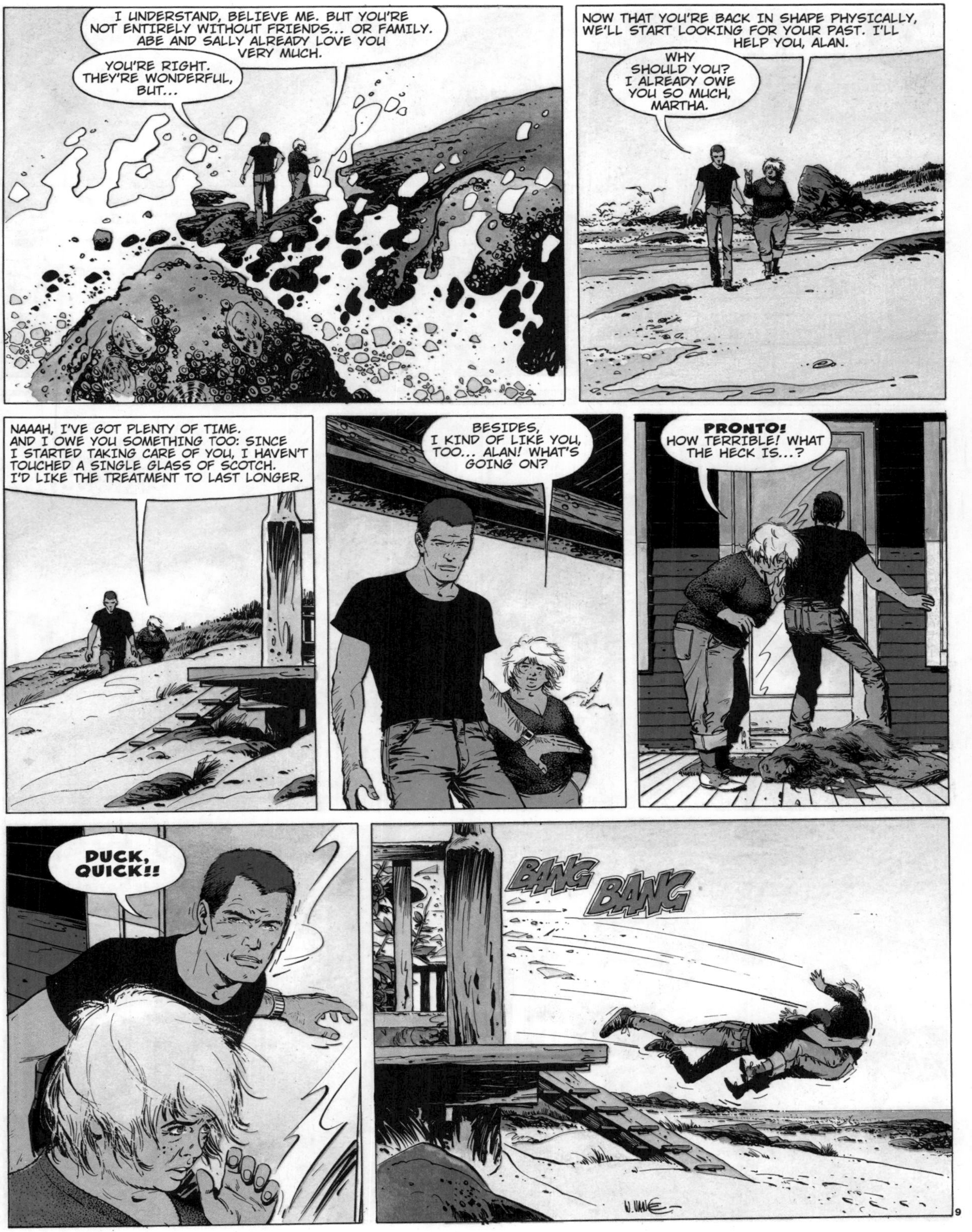
I UNDERSTAND, BELIEVE ME. BUT YOU'RE NOT ENTIRELY WITHOUT FRIENDS... OR FAMILY. ABE AND SALLY ALREADY LOVE YOU VERY MUCH.
YOU'RE RIGHT. THEY'RE WONDERFUL, BUT...
NOW THAT YOU'RE BACK IN SHAPE PHYSICALLY, WE'LL START LOOKING FOR YOUR PAST. I'LL HELP YOU, ALAN.
WHY SHOULD YOU? I ALREADY OWE YOU SO MUCH, MARTHA.
NAAAH, I'VE GOT PLENTY OF TIME. AND I OWE YOU SOMETHING TOO: SINCE I STARTED TAKING CARE OF YOU, I HAVEN'T TOUCHED A SINGLE GLASS OF SCOTCH. I'D LIKE THE TREATMENT TO LAST LONGER.
BESIDES, I KIND OF LIKE YOU, TOO... ALAN! WHAT'S GOING ON?
PRONTO! HOW TERRIBLE! WHAT THE HECK IS...?
DUCK, QUICK!!
BANG
BANG
9

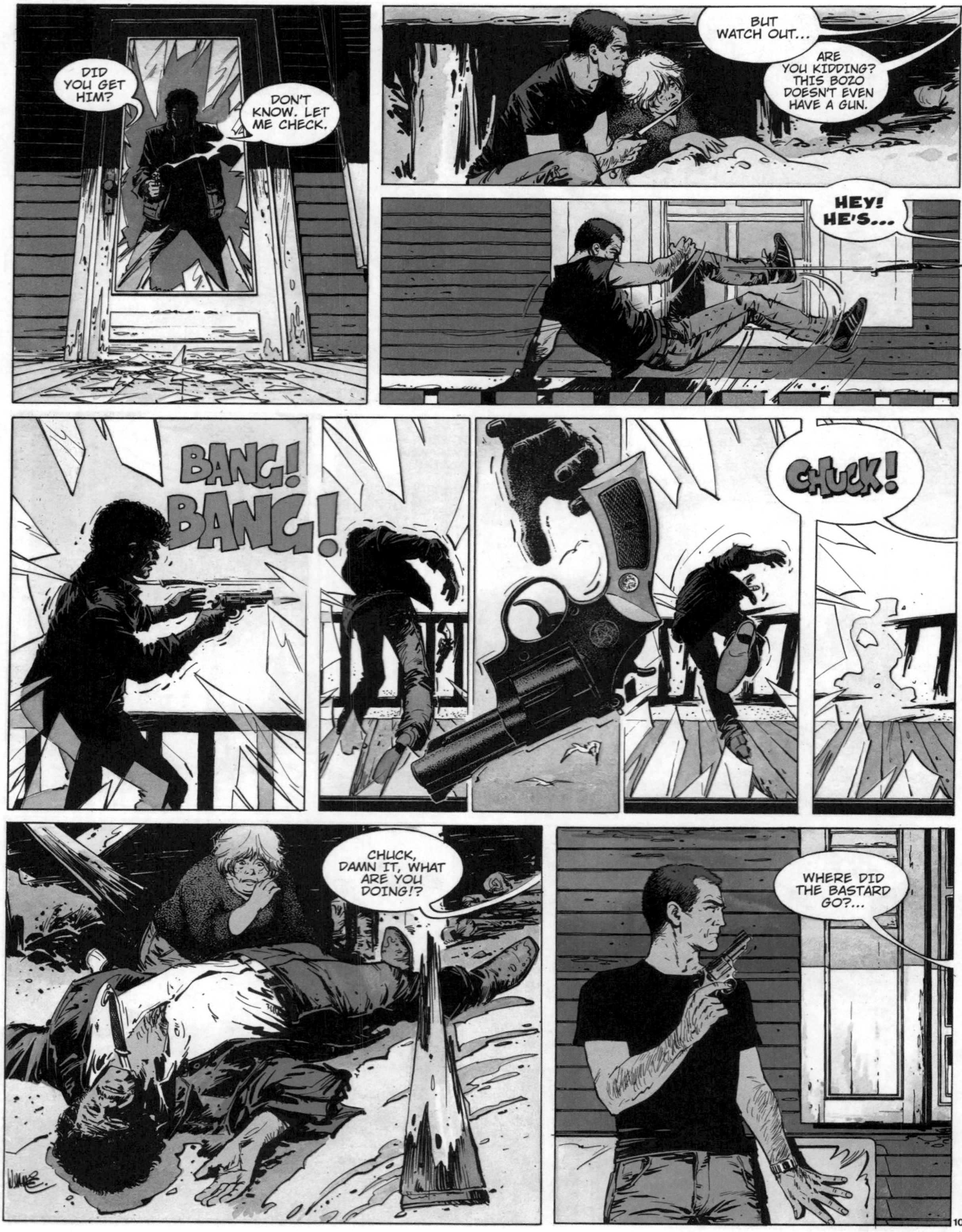
DID YOU GET HIM?
DON'T KNOW. LET ME CHECK.
BUT WATCH OUT...
ARE YOU KIDDING? THIS BOZO DOESN'T EVEN HAVE A GUN.
HEY! HE'S...
BANG! BANG!
CHUCK!
CHUCK, DAMN IT, WHAT ARE YOU DOING!?
WHERE DID THE BASTARD GO?...
10

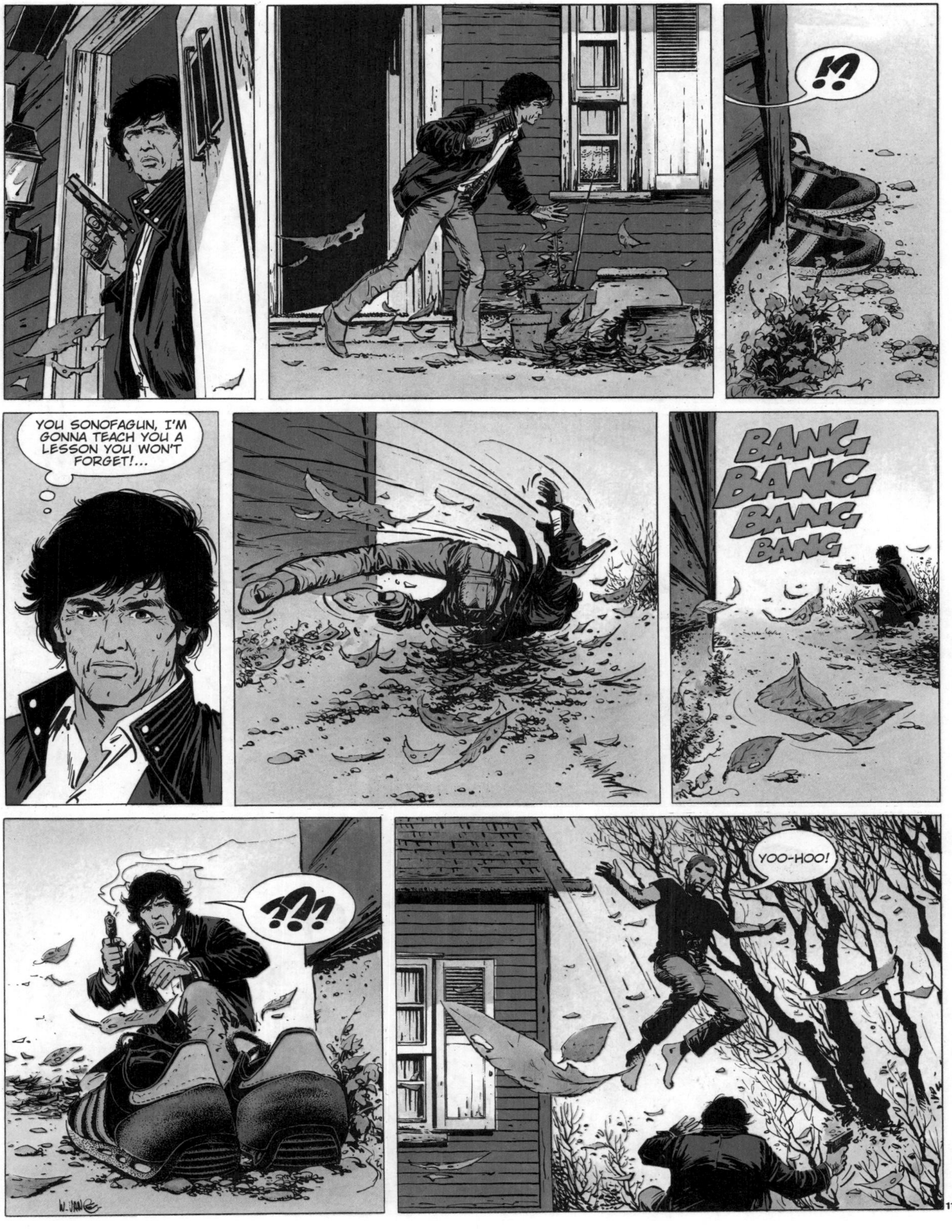
!?
YOU SONOFAGUN, I'M GONNA TEACH YOU A LESSON YOU WON'T FORGET!...
BANG BANG BANG BANG
?!?!
YOO-HOO!
W. VANCE
11

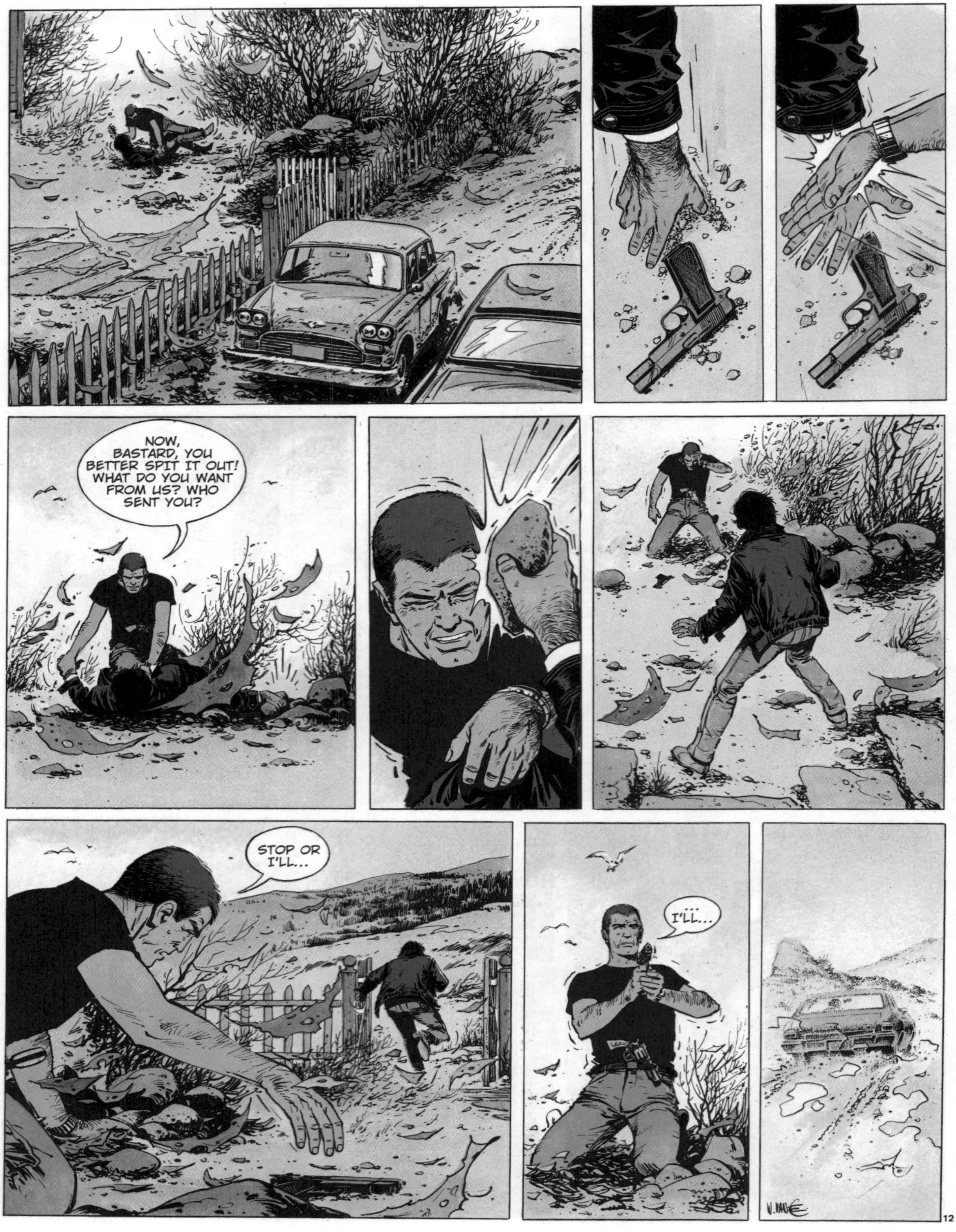
NOW, BASTARD, YOU BETTER SPIT IT OUT! WHAT DO YOU WANT FROM US? WHO SENT YOU?
STOP OR I'LL...
... I'LL...
12

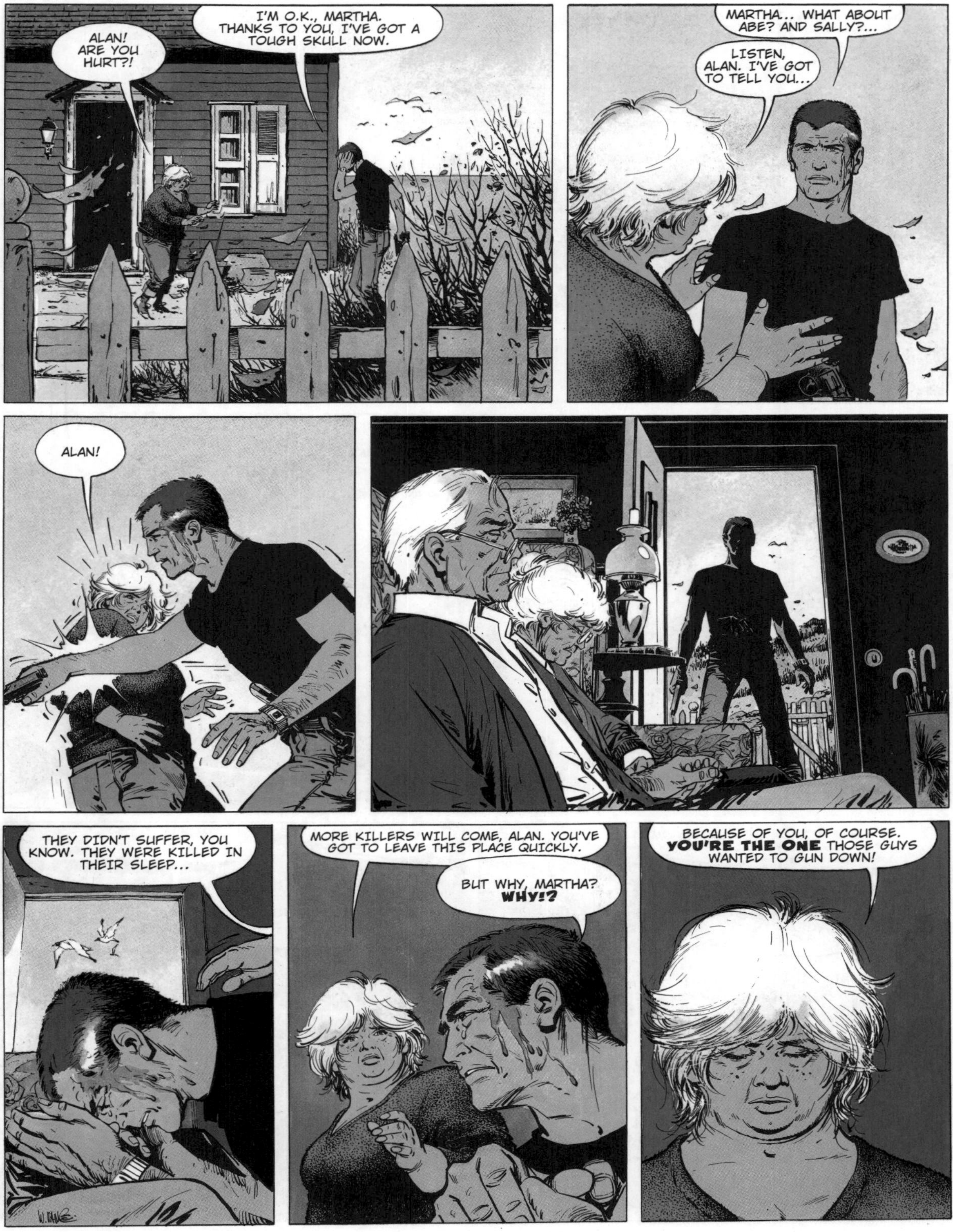
ALAN! ARE YOU HURT?!
I'M O.K., MARTHA. THANKS TO YOU, I'VE GOT A TOUGH SKULL NOW.
MARTHA... WHAT ABOUT ABE? AND SALLY?...
LISTEN, ALAN. I'VE GOT TO TELL YOU...
ALAN!
THEY DIDN'T SUFFER, YOU KNOW. THEY WERE KILLED IN THEIR SLEEP...
MORE KILLERS WILL COME, ALAN. YOU'VE GOT TO LEAVE THIS PLACE QUICKLY.
BUT WHY, MARTHA? **WHY!?**
BECAUSE OF YOU, OF COURSE. **YOU'RE THE ONE** THOSE GUYS WANTED TO GUN DOWN!

13

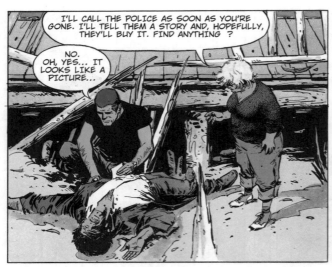

I'LL CALL THE POLICE AS SOON AS YOU'RE GONE. I'LL TELL THEM A STORY AND, HOPEFULLY, THEY'LL BUY IT. FIND ANYTHING ?

NO. OH, YES... IT LOOKS LIKE A PICTURE...

OH, MY GOD!...

HE HAD IT WITH HIM TO IDENTIFY YOU; THAT MUCH IS OBVIOUS. SO, THESE TWO MEN DIDN'T KNOW YOU. AS FOR THIS YOUNG WOMAN... SHE'S BEAUTIFUL. WHO IS SHE?

HOW DO YOU EXPECT ME TO KNOW, MARTHA?

SHE MAY BE MY WIFE, MY SISTER, A FRIEND... HER FACE DOESN'T REMIND ME OF ANYTHING... LIKE ALL THE REST.

ALAN, LOOK...

THE PHOTOGRAPHER'S NAME IS ON THE BACK.

PHOTO - CINE BARNES 722 23d street - EASTOWN -

EASTOWN? WHAT'S THAT?

A BIG CITY ON THE COAST, SOME 200 MILES FROM HERE.

THEN I'LL START WITH EASTOWN. ABE'S CAR SHOULD BE ABLE TO TAKE ME THAT FAR.

BUT YOU'LL BE LEAPING STRAIGHT INTO THE LION'S DEN!

THAT'S EXACTLY WHAT I'M HOPING, MARTHA. HOW ELSE CAN I FIND OUT **WHO** I AM THAT SOMEONE'S TRYING TO KILL ME?

14

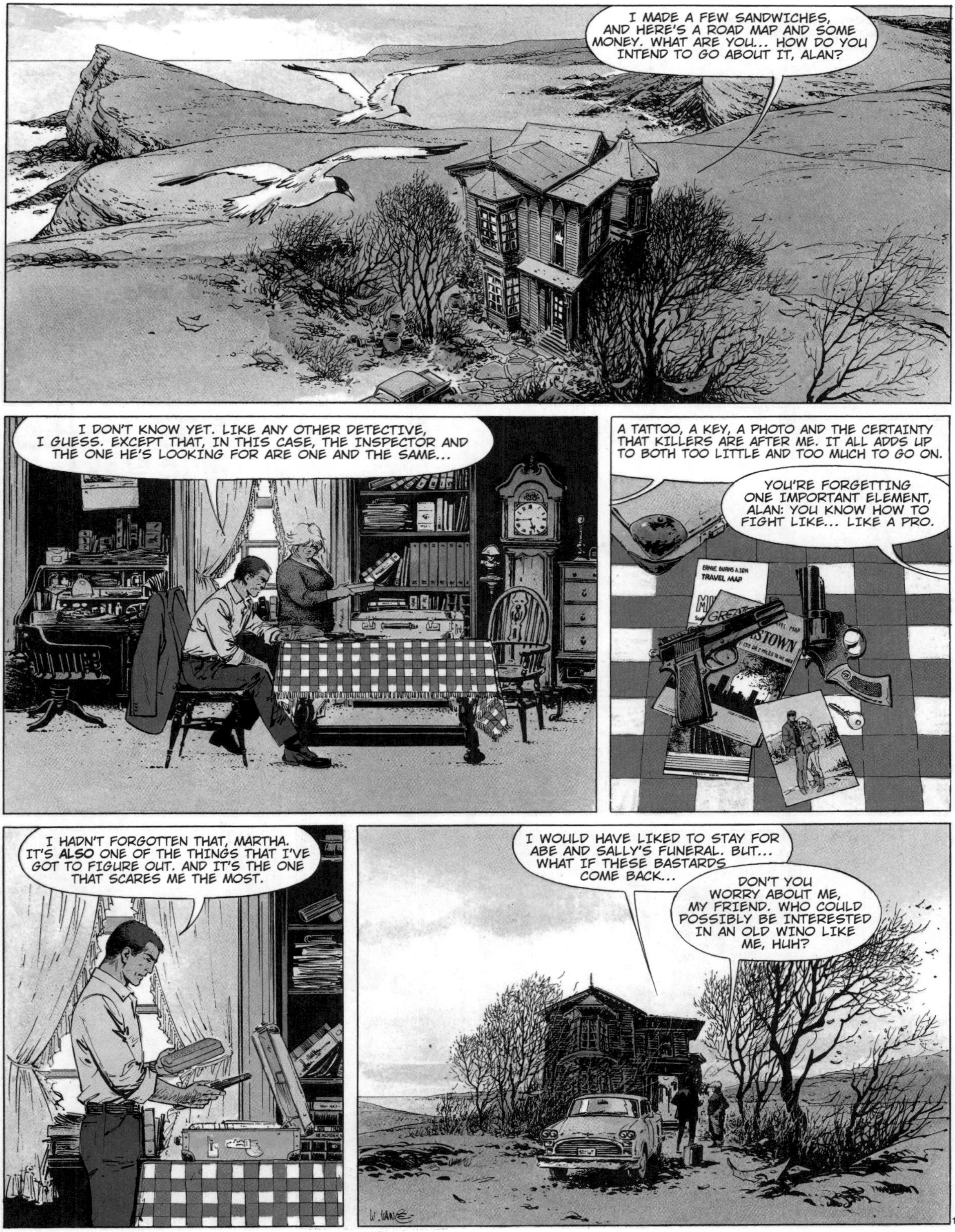
I MADE A FEW SANDWICHES, AND HERE'S A ROAD MAP AND SOME MONEY. WHAT ARE YOU... HOW DO YOU INTEND TO GO ABOUT IT, ALAN?
I DON'T KNOW YET. LIKE ANY OTHER DETECTIVE, I GUESS. EXCEPT THAT, IN THIS CASE, THE INSPECTOR AND THE ONE HE'S LOOKING FOR ARE ONE AND THE SAME...
A TATTOO, A KEY, A PHOTO AND THE CERTAINTY THAT KILLERS ARE AFTER ME. IT ALL ADDS UP TO BOTH TOO LITTLE AND TOO MUCH TO GO ON.
YOU'RE FORGETTING ONE IMPORTANT ELEMENT, ALAN: YOU KNOW HOW TO FIGHT LIKE... LIKE A PRO.
ERNIE BURNS & SON
TRAVEL MAP
I HADN'T FORGOTTEN THAT, MARTHA. IT'S **ALSO** ONE OF THE THINGS THAT I'VE GOT TO FIGURE OUT. AND IT'S THE ONE THAT SCARES ME THE MOST.
I WOULD HAVE LIKED TO STAY FOR ABE AND SALLY'S FUNERAL. BUT... WHAT IF THESE BASTARDS COME BACK...
DON'T YOU WORRY ABOUT ME, MY FRIEND. WHO COULD POSSIBLY BE INTERESTED IN AN OLD WINO LIKE ME, HUH?
W. VANCE
15

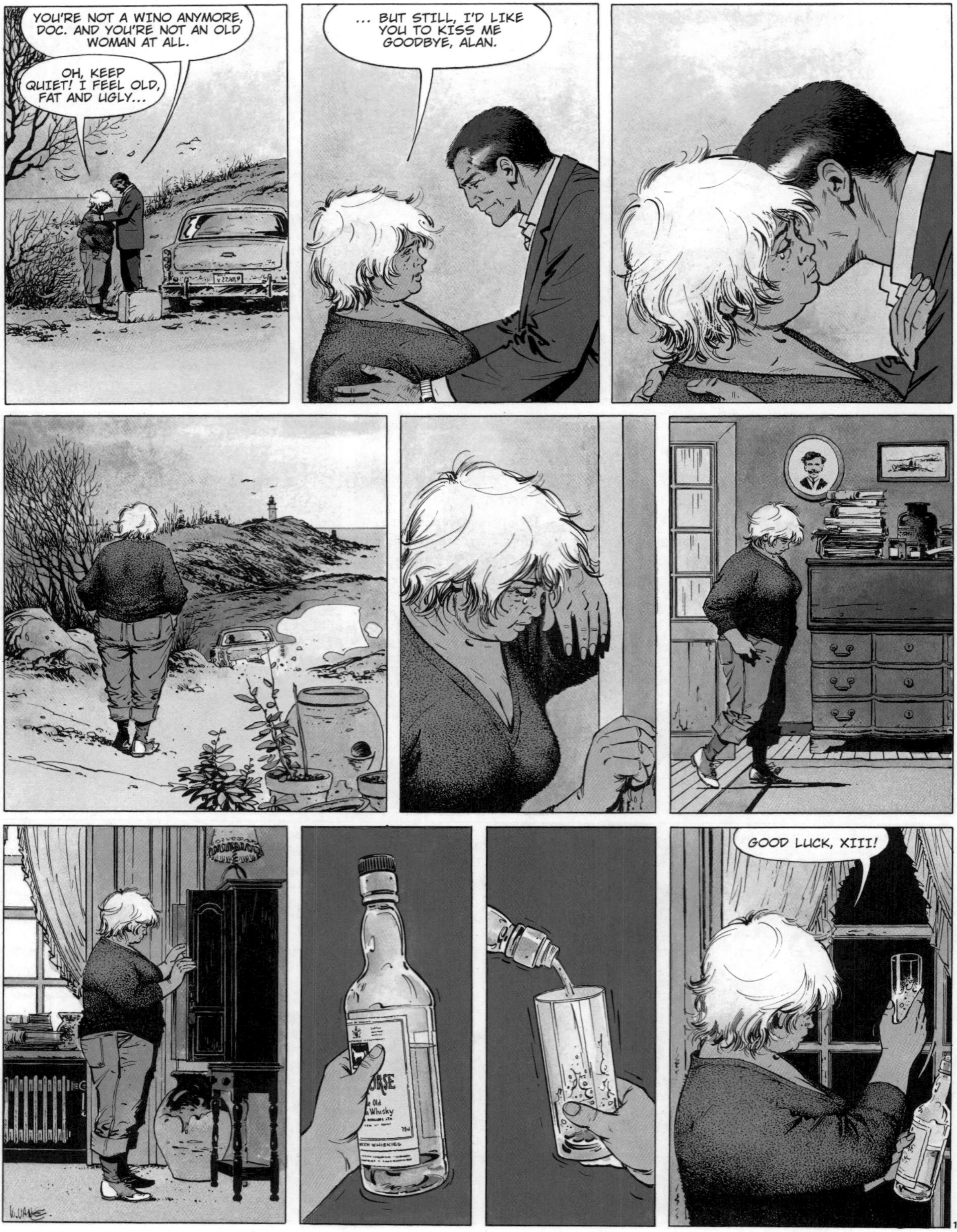
YOU'RE NOT A WINO ANYMORE, DOC. AND YOU'RE NOT AN OLD WOMAN AT ALL.
OH, KEEP QUIET! I FEEL OLD, FAT AND UGLY...
... BUT STILL, I'D LIKE YOU TO KISS ME GOODBYE, ALAN.
GOOD LUCK, XIII!
16

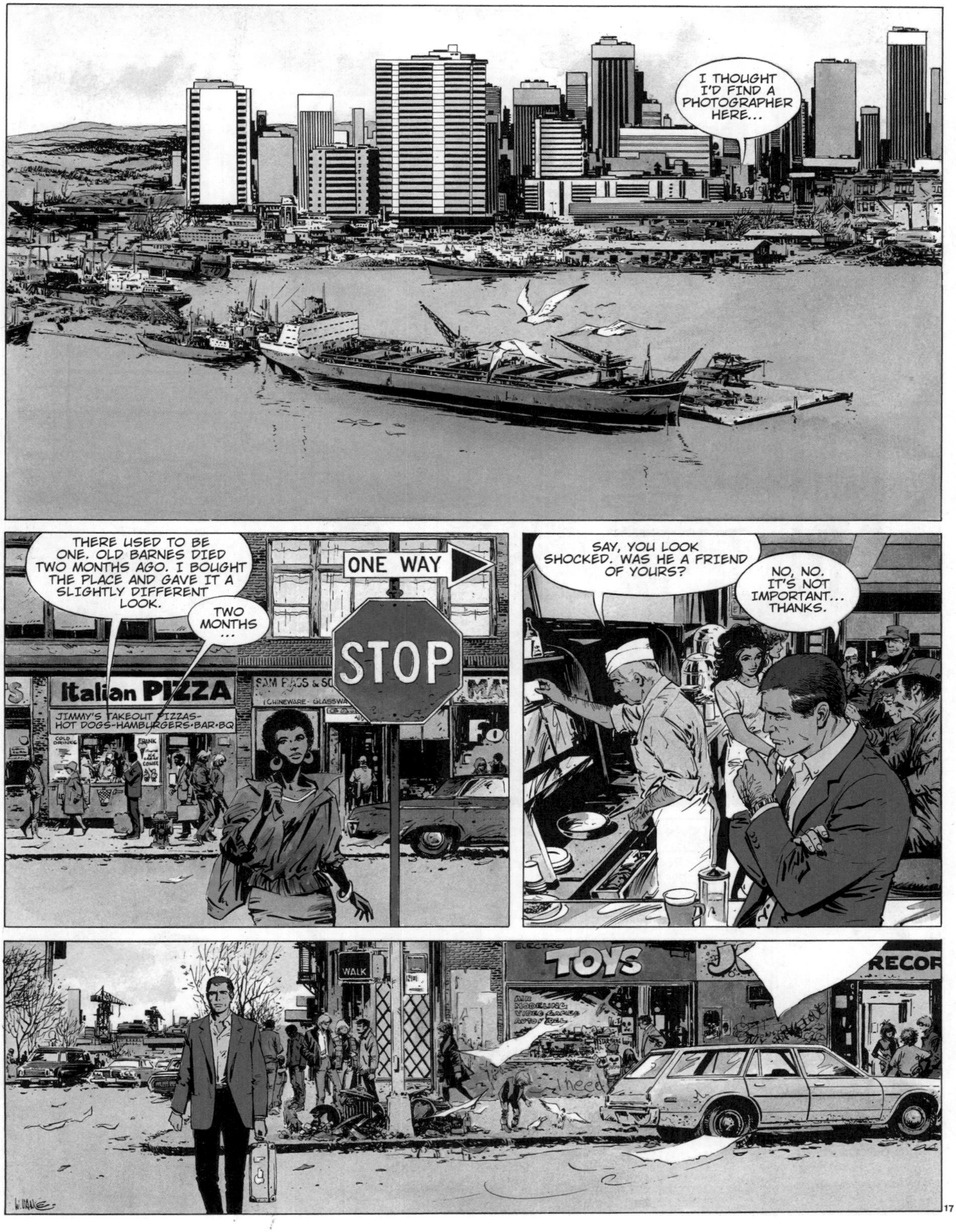
I THOUGHT I'D FIND A PHOTOGRAPHER HERE...
THERE USED TO BE ONE. OLD BARNES DIED TWO MONTHS AGO. I BOUGHT THE PLACE AND GAVE IT A SLIGHTLY DIFFERENT LOOK.
TWO MONTHS ...
ONE WAY
STOP
Italian PIZZA
JIMMY'S TAKEOUT PIZZAS-HOT DOGS-HAMBURGERS-BAR-BQ
SAY, YOU LOOK SHOCKED. WAS HE A FRIEND OF YOURS?
NO, NO. IT'S NOT IMPORTANT... THANKS.
WALK
TOYS
17

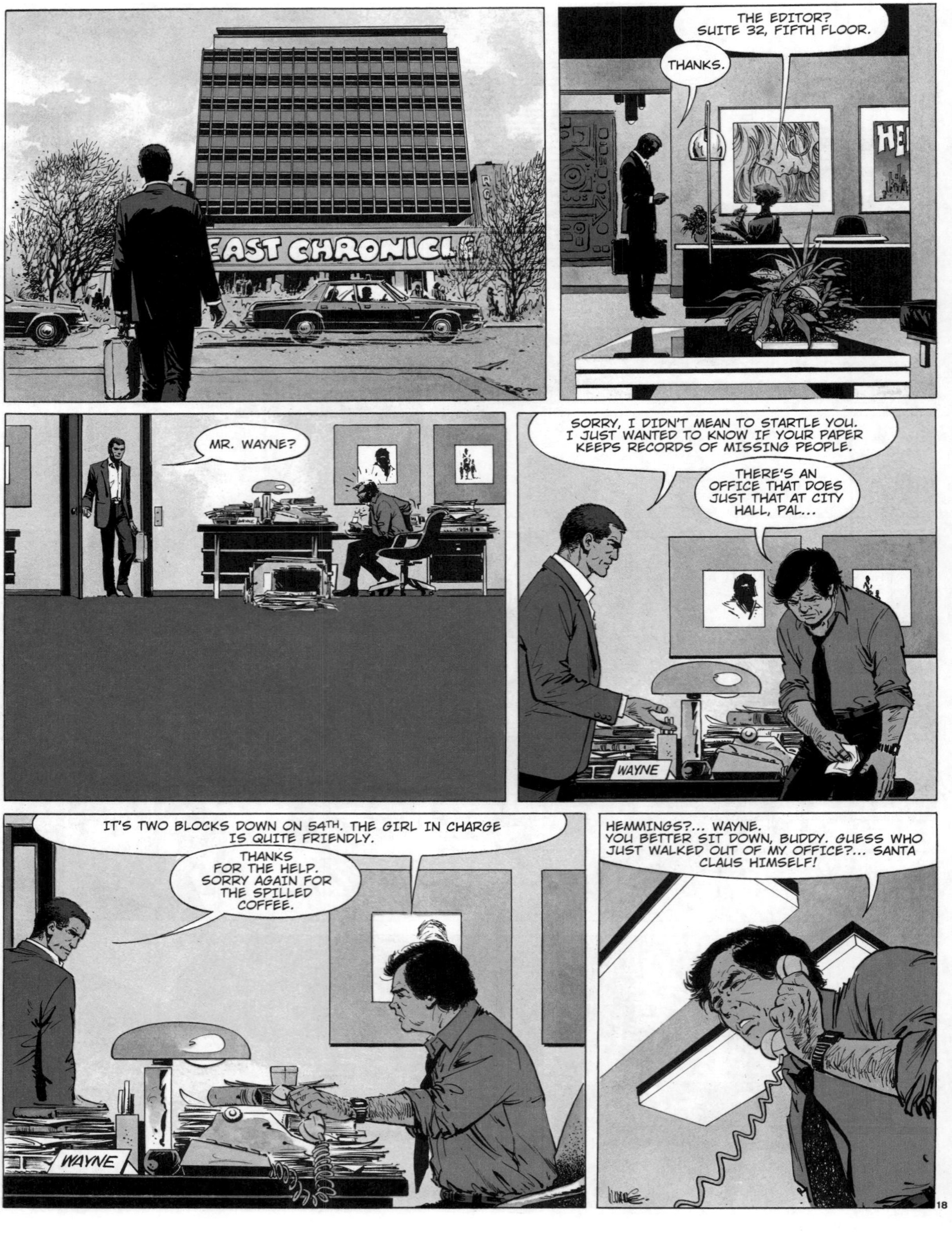
EAST CHRONICLE
THE EDITOR? SUITE 32, FIFTH FLOOR.
THANKS.
MR. WAYNE?
SORRY, I DIDN'T MEAN TO STARTLE YOU. I JUST WANTED TO KNOW IF YOUR PAPER KEEPS RECORDS OF MISSING PEOPLE.
THERE'S AN OFFICE THAT DOES JUST THAT AT CITY HALL, PAL...
WAYNE
IT'S TWO BLOCKS DOWN ON 54TH. THE GIRL IN CHARGE IS QUITE FRIENDLY.
THANKS FOR THE HELP. SORRY AGAIN FOR THE SPILLED COFFEE.
WAYNE
HEMMINGS?... WAYNE. YOU BETTER SIT DOWN, BUDDY. GUESS WHO JUST WALKED OUT OF MY OFFICE?... SANTA CLAUS HIMSELF!
18

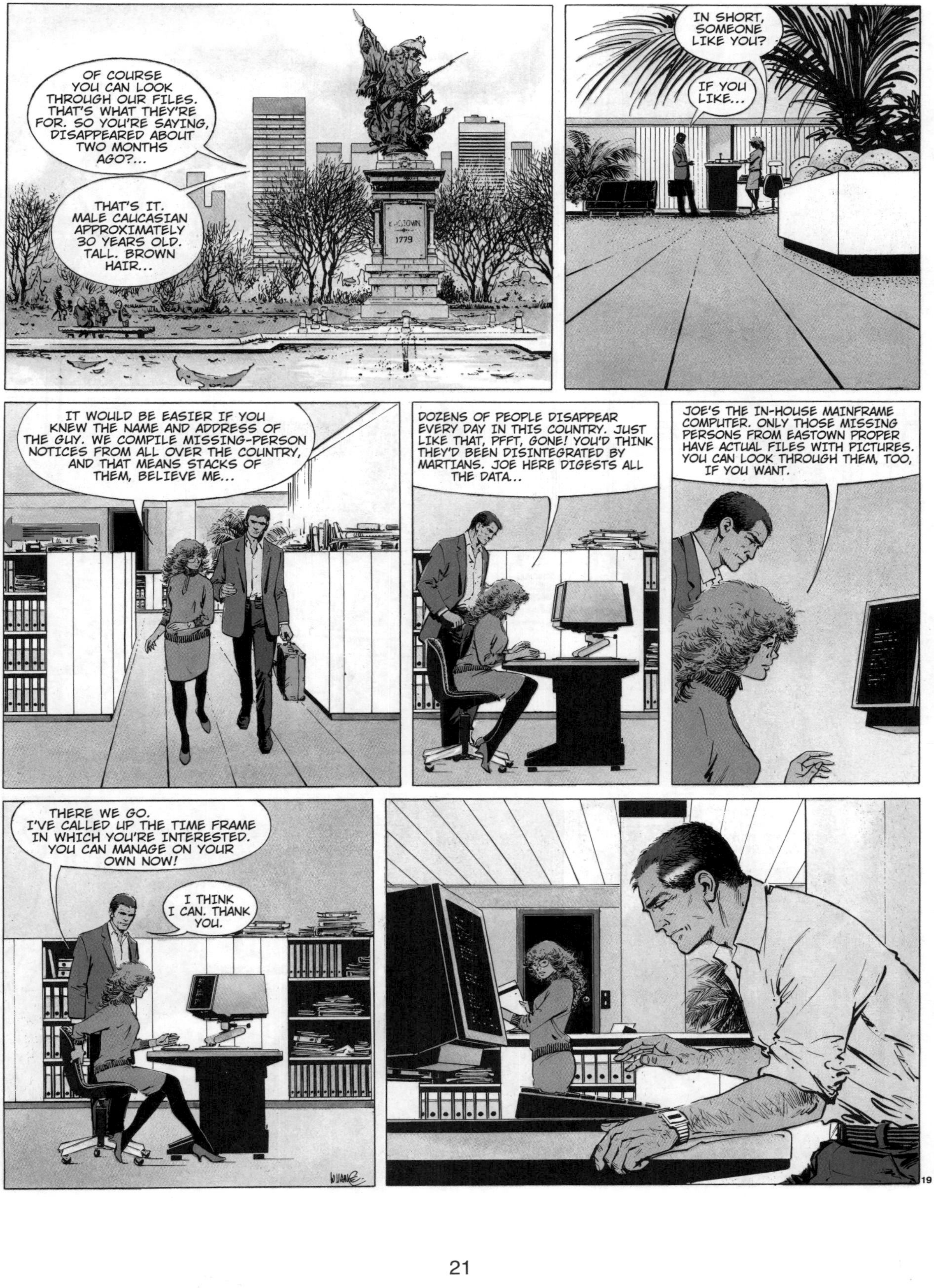
OF COURSE YOU CAN LOOK THROUGH OUR FILES. THAT'S WHAT THEY'RE FOR. SO YOU'RE SAYING, DISAPPEARED ABOUT TWO MONTHS AGO?...
THAT'S IT. MALE CAUCASIAN APPROXIMATELY 30 YEARS OLD. TALL. BROWN HAIR...
1779
IN SHORT, SOMEONE LIKE YOU?
IF YOU LIKE...
IT WOULD BE EASIER IF YOU KNEW THE NAME AND ADDRESS OF THE GUY. WE COMPILE MISSING-PERSON NOTICES FROM ALL OVER THE COUNTRY, AND THAT MEANS STACKS OF THEM, BELIEVE ME...
DOZENS OF PEOPLE DISAPPEAR EVERY DAY IN THIS COUNTRY. JUST LIKE THAT, PFFT, GONE! YOU'D THINK THEY'D BEEN DISINTEGRATED BY MARTIANS. JOE HERE DIGESTS ALL THE DATA...
JOE'S THE IN-HOUSE MAINFRAME COMPUTER. ONLY THOSE MISSING PERSONS FROM EASTOWN PROPER HAVE ACTUAL FILES WITH PICTURES. YOU CAN LOOK THROUGH THEM, TOO, IF YOU WANT.
THERE WE GO. I'VE CALLED UP THE TIME FRAME IN WHICH YOU'RE INTERESTED. YOU CAN MANAGE ON YOUR OWN NOW!
I THINK I CAN. THANK YOU.
19

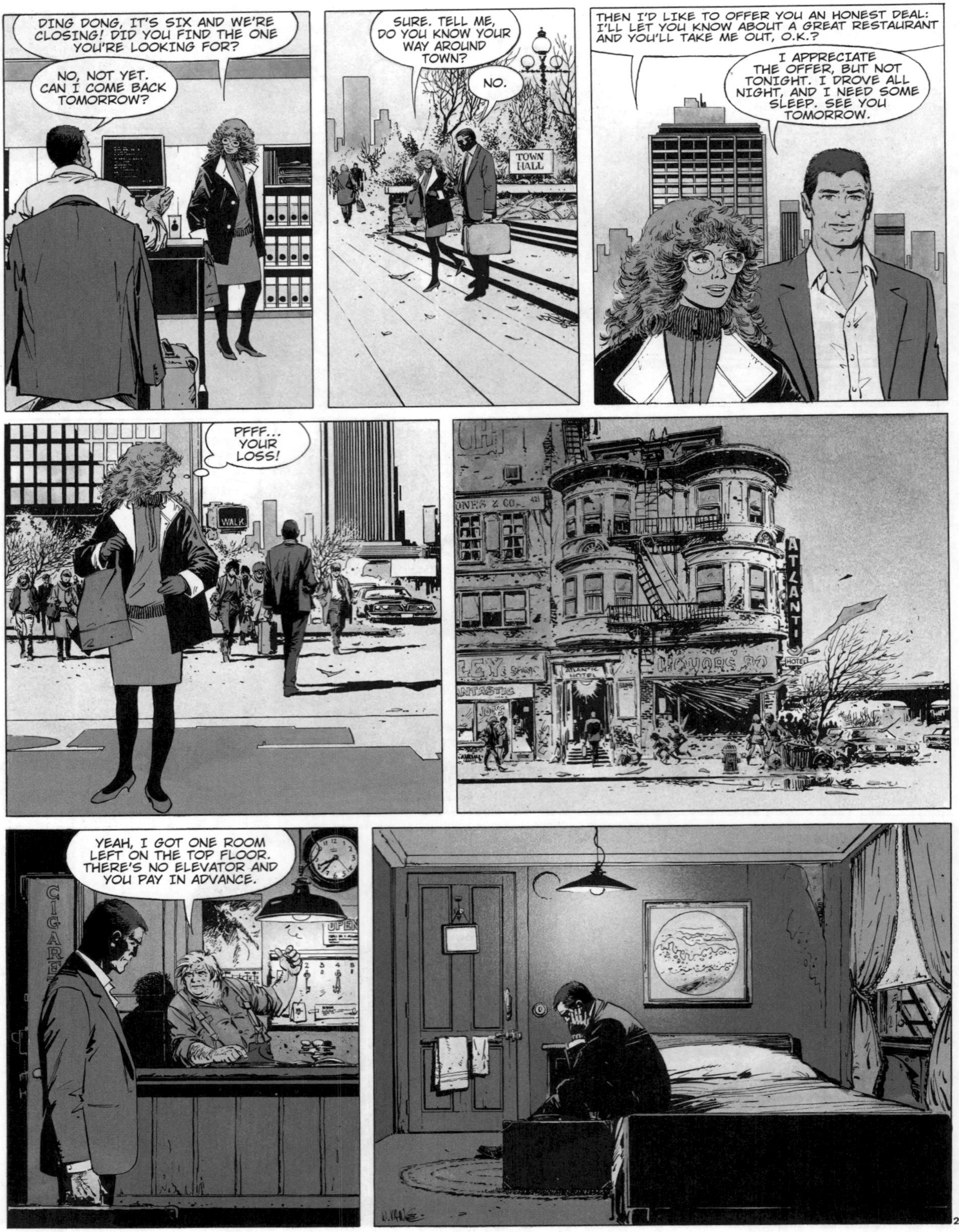
DING DONG, IT'S SIX AND WE'RE CLOSING! DID YOU FIND THE ONE YOU'RE LOOKING FOR?
NO, NOT YET. CAN I COME BACK TOMORROW?
SURE. TELL ME, DO YOU KNOW YOUR WAY AROUND TOWN?
NO.
TOWN HALL
THEN I'D LIKE TO OFFER YOU AN HONEST DEAL: I'LL LET YOU KNOW ABOUT A GREAT RESTAURANT AND YOU'LL TAKE ME OUT, O.K.?
I APPRECIATE THE OFFER, BUT NOT TONIGHT. I DROVE ALL NIGHT, AND I NEED SOME SLEEP. SEE YOU TOMORROW.
PFFF... YOUR LOSS!
WALK
ATLANTIC HOTEL
HOTEL
YEAH, I GOT ONE ROOM LEFT ON THE TOP FLOOR. THERE'S NO ELEVATOR AND YOU PAY IN ADVANCE.
20

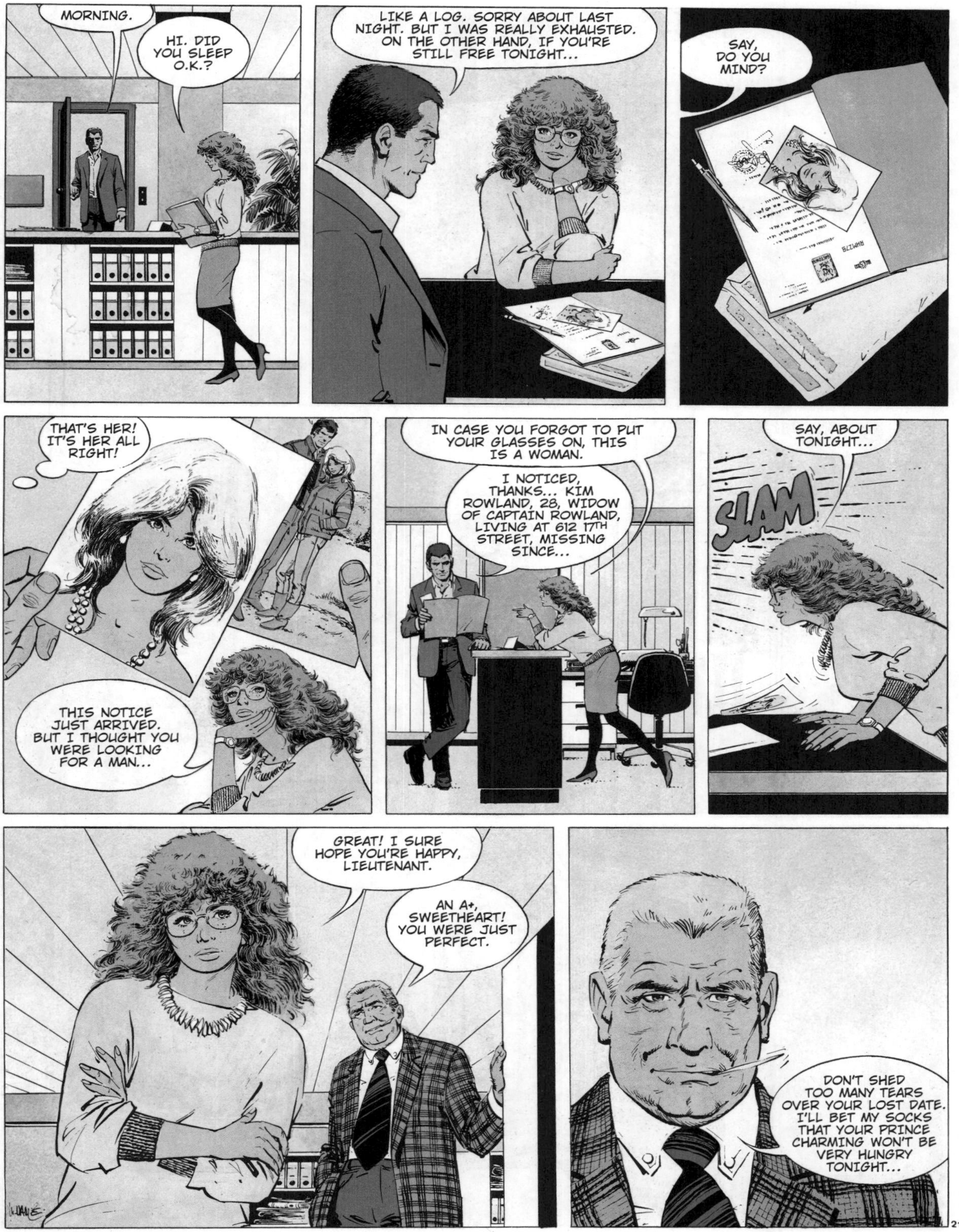
MORNING.
HI. DID YOU SLEEP O.K.?
LIKE A LOG. SORRY ABOUT LAST NIGHT. BUT I WAS REALLY EXHAUSTED. ON THE OTHER HAND, IF YOU'RE STILL FREE TONIGHT...
SAY, DO YOU MIND?
THAT'S HER! IT'S HER ALL RIGHT!
THIS NOTICE JUST ARRIVED. BUT I THOUGHT YOU WERE LOOKING FOR A MAN...
IN CASE YOU FORGOT TO PUT YOUR GLASSES ON, THIS IS A WOMAN.
I NOTICED, THANKS... KIM ROWLAND, 28, WIDOW OF CAPTAIN ROWLAND, LIVING AT 612 17TH STREET, MISSING SINCE...
SAY, ABOUT TONIGHT...
SLAM
GREAT! I SURE HOPE YOU'RE HAPPY, LIEUTENANT.
AN A+, SWEETHEART! YOU WERE JUST PERFECT.
DON'T SHED TOO MANY TEARS OVER YOUR LOST DATE. I'LL BET MY SOCKS THAT YOUR PRINCE CHARMING WON'T BE VERY HUNGRY TONIGHT...
21

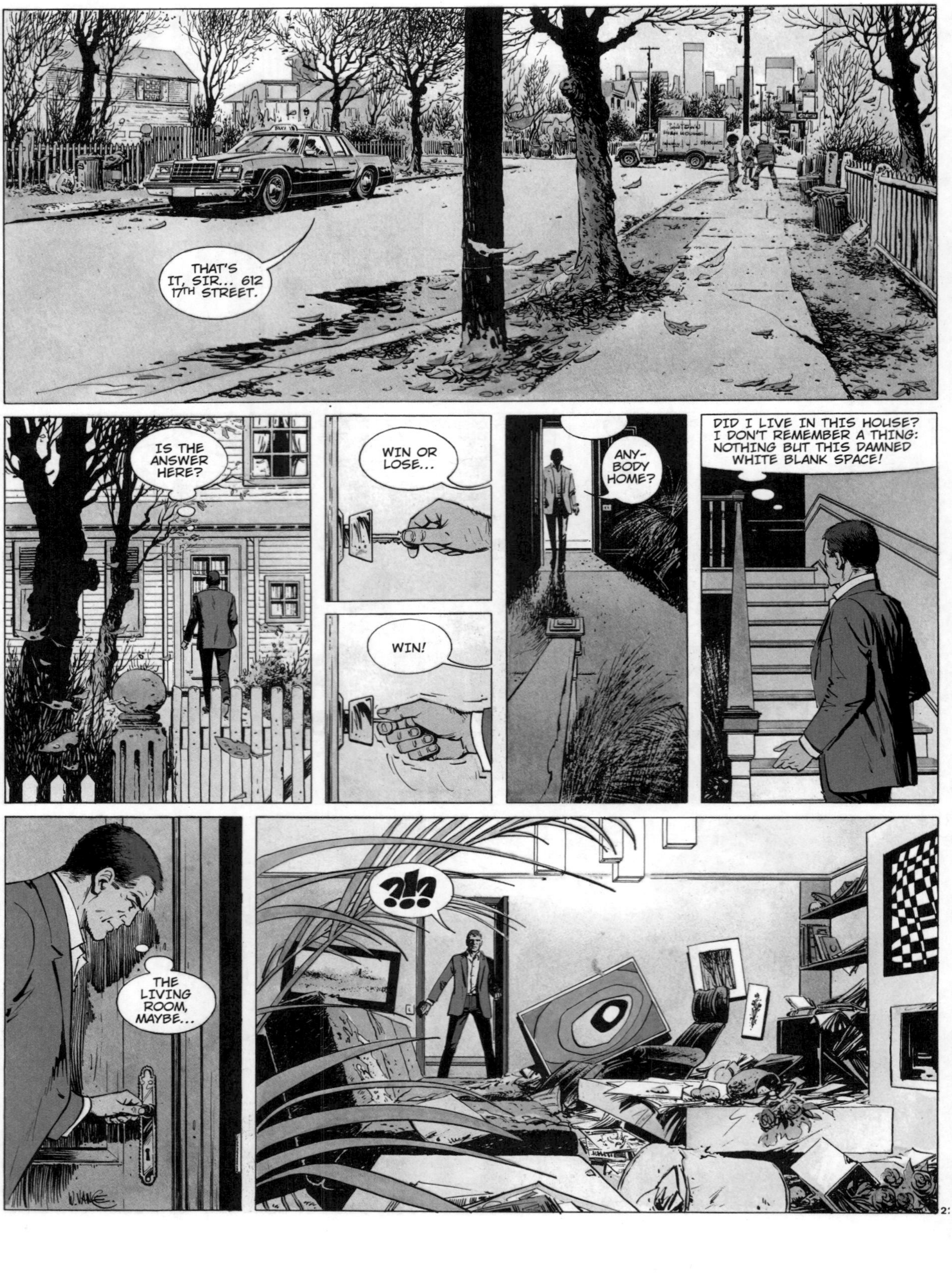
THAT'S IT, SIR... 612 17TH STREET.
IS THE ANSWER HERE?
WIN OR LOSE...
WIN!
ANY-BODY HOME?
DID I LIVE IN THIS HOUSE? I DON'T REMEMBER A THING: NOTHING BUT THIS DAMNED WHITE BLANK SPACE!
THE LIVING ROOM, MAYBE...
?!!?

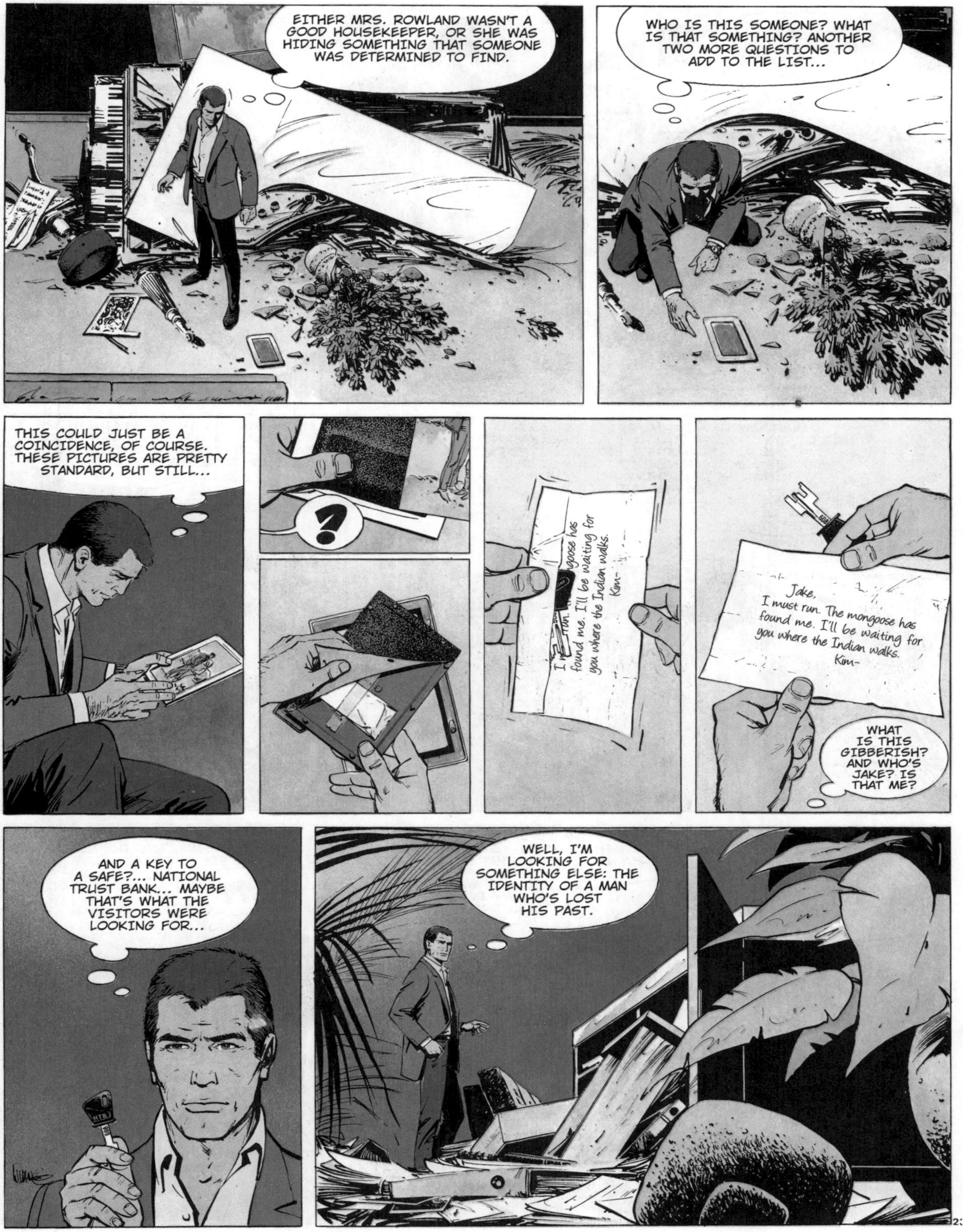
EITHER MRS. ROWLAND WASN'T A GOOD HOUSEKEEPER, OR SHE WAS HIDING SOMETHING THAT SOMEONE WAS DETERMINED TO FIND.
WHO IS THIS SOMEONE? WHAT IS THAT SOMETHING? ANOTHER TWO MORE QUESTIONS TO ADD TO THE LIST...
THIS COULD JUST BE A COINCIDENCE, OF COURSE. THESE PICTURES ARE PRETTY STANDARD, BUT STILL...
!
Jake,
I must run. The mongoose has found me. I'll be waiting for you where the Indian walks.
Kim-
WHAT IS THIS GIBBERISH? AND WHO'S JAKE? IS THAT ME?
AND A KEY TO A SAFE?... NATIONAL TRUST BANK... MAYBE THAT'S WHAT THE VISITORS WERE LOOKING FOR...
WELL, I'M LOOKING FOR SOMETHING ELSE: THE IDENTITY OF A MAN WHO'S LOST HIS PAST.

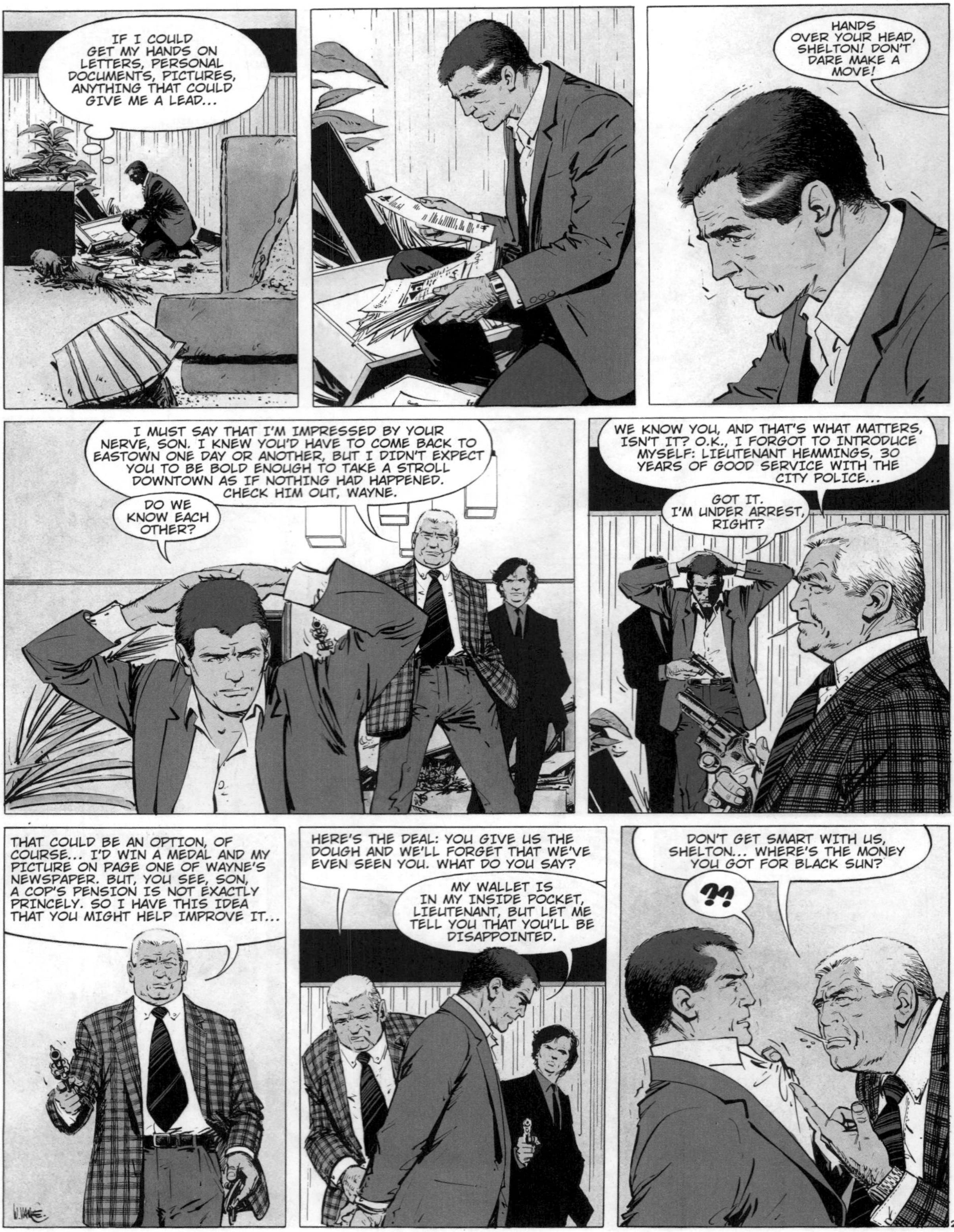
IF I COULD GET MY HANDS ON LETTERS, PERSONAL DOCUMENTS, PICTURES, ANYTHING THAT COULD GIVE ME A LEAD...
HANDS OVER YOUR HEAD, SHELTON! DON'T DARE MAKE A MOVE!
I MUST SAY THAT I'M IMPRESSED BY YOUR NERVE, SON. I KNEW YOU'D HAVE TO COME BACK TO EASTOWN ONE DAY OR ANOTHER, BUT I DIDN'T EXPECT YOU TO BE BOLD ENOUGH TO TAKE A STROLL DOWNTOWN AS IF NOTHING HAD HAPPENED. CHECK HIM OUT, WAYNE.
DO WE KNOW EACH OTHER?
WE KNOW YOU, AND THAT'S WHAT MATTERS, ISN'T IT? O.K., I FORGOT TO INTRODUCE MYSELF: LIEUTENANT HEMMINGS, 30 YEARS OF GOOD SERVICE WITH THE CITY POLICE...
GOT IT. I'M UNDER ARREST, RIGHT?
THAT COULD BE AN OPTION, OF COURSE... I'D WIN A MEDAL AND MY PICTURE ON PAGE ONE OF WAYNE'S NEWSPAPER. BUT, YOU SEE, SON, A COP'S PENSION IS NOT EXACTLY PRINCELY. SO I HAVE THIS IDEA THAT YOU MIGHT HELP IMPROVE IT...
HERE'S THE DEAL: YOU GIVE US THE DOUGH AND WE'LL FORGET THAT WE'VE EVEN SEEN YOU. WHAT DO YOU SAY?
MY WALLET IS IN MY INSIDE POCKET, LIEUTENANT, BUT LET ME TELL YOU THAT YOU'LL BE DISAPPOINTED.
DON'T GET SMART WITH US, SHELTON... WHERE'S THE MONEY YOU GOT FOR BLACK SUN?
??
24

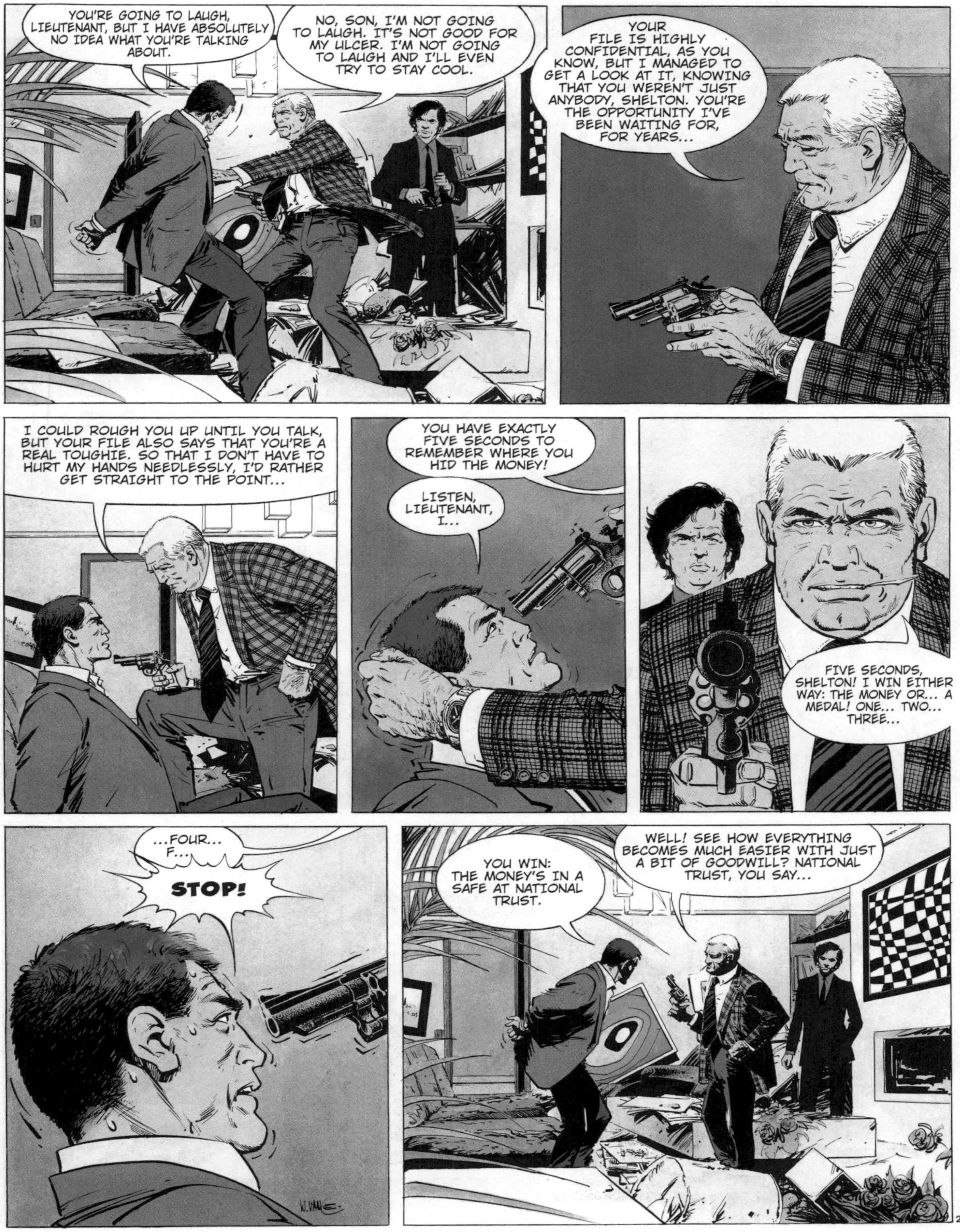
YOU'RE GOING TO LAUGH, LIEUTENANT, BUT I HAVE ABSOLUTELY NO IDEA WHAT YOU'RE TALKING ABOUT.
NO, SON, I'M NOT GOING TO LAUGH. IT'S NOT GOOD FOR MY ULCER. I'M NOT GOING TO LAUGH AND I'LL EVEN TRY TO STAY COOL.
YOUR FILE IS HIGHLY CONFIDENTIAL, AS YOU KNOW, BUT I MANAGED TO GET A LOOK AT IT, KNOWING THAT YOU WEREN'T JUST ANYBODY, SHELTON. YOU'RE THE OPPORTUNITY I'VE BEEN WAITING FOR, FOR YEARS...
I COULD ROUGH YOU UP UNTIL YOU TALK, BUT YOUR FILE ALSO SAYS THAT YOU'RE A REAL TOUGHIE. SO THAT I DON'T HAVE TO HURT MY HANDS NEEDLESSLY, I'D RATHER GET STRAIGHT TO THE POINT...
YOU HAVE EXACTLY FIVE SECONDS TO REMEMBER WHERE YOU HID THE MONEY!
LISTEN, LIEUTENANT, I...
FIVE SECONDS, SHELTON! I WIN EITHER WAY: THE MONEY OR... A MEDAL! ONE... TWO... THREE...
...FOUR... F...
STOP!
W. VANCE
YOU WIN: THE MONEY'S IN A SAFE AT NATIONAL TRUST.
WELL! SEE HOW EVERYTHING BECOMES MUCH EASIER WITH JUST A BIT OF GOODWILL? NATIONAL TRUST, YOU SAY...
25

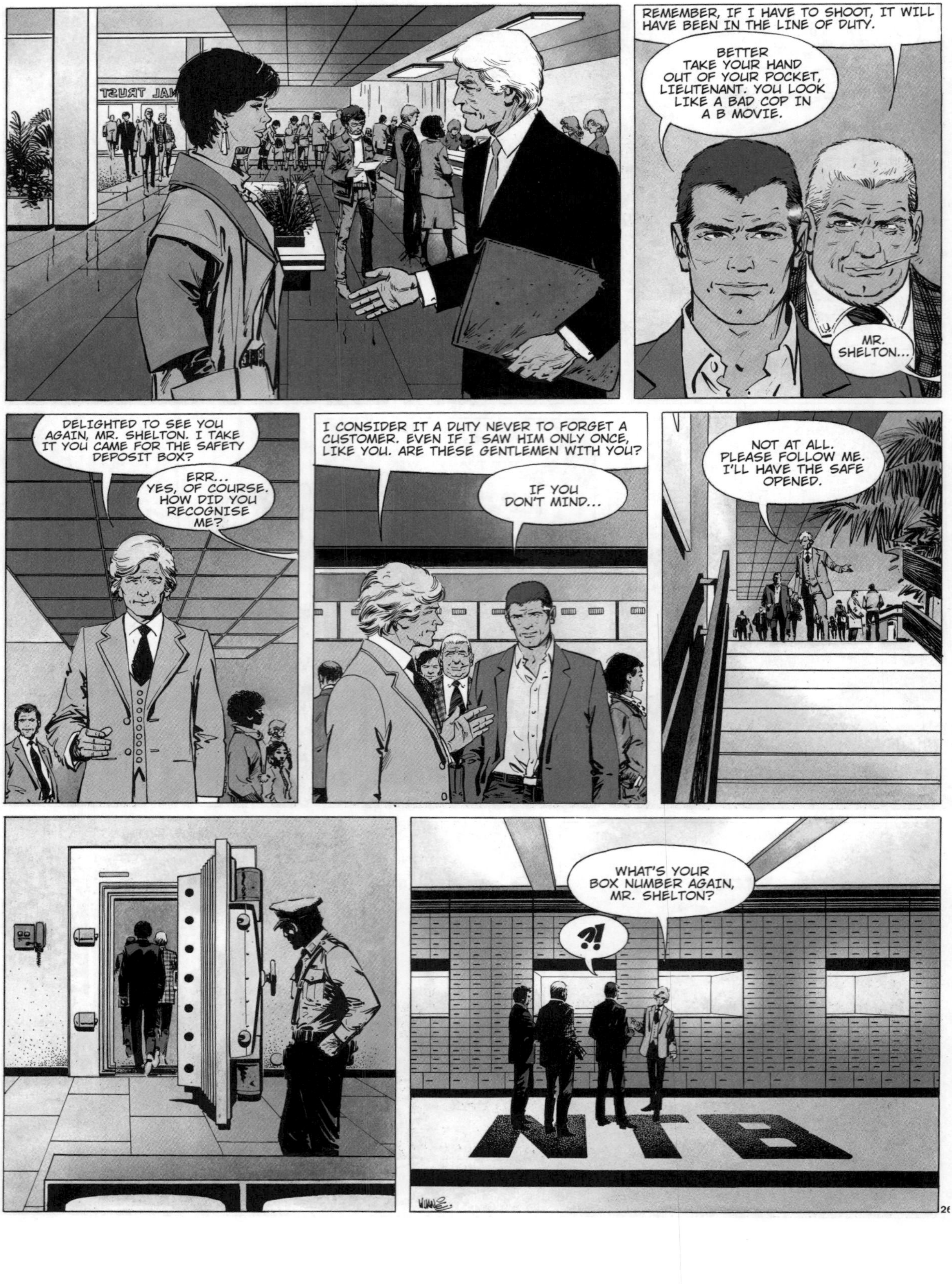
NAL TRUST
REMEMBER, IF I HAVE TO SHOOT, IT WILL HAVE BEEN IN THE LINE OF DUTY.
BETTER TAKE YOUR HAND OUT OF YOUR POCKET, LIEUTENANT. YOU LOOK LIKE A BAD COP IN A B MOVIE.
MR. SHELTON...
DELIGHTED TO SEE YOU AGAIN, MR. SHELTON. I TAKE IT YOU CAME FOR THE SAFETY DEPOSIT BOX?
ERR... YES, OF COURSE. HOW DID YOU RECOGNISE ME?
I CONSIDER IT A DUTY NEVER TO FORGET A CUSTOMER. EVEN IF I SAW HIM ONLY ONCE, LIKE YOU. ARE THESE GENTLEMEN WITH YOU?
IF YOU DON'T MIND...
NOT AT ALL. PLEASE FOLLOW ME. I'LL HAVE THE SAFE OPENED.
WHAT'S YOUR BOX NUMBER AGAIN, MR. SHELTON?
?!
NIB

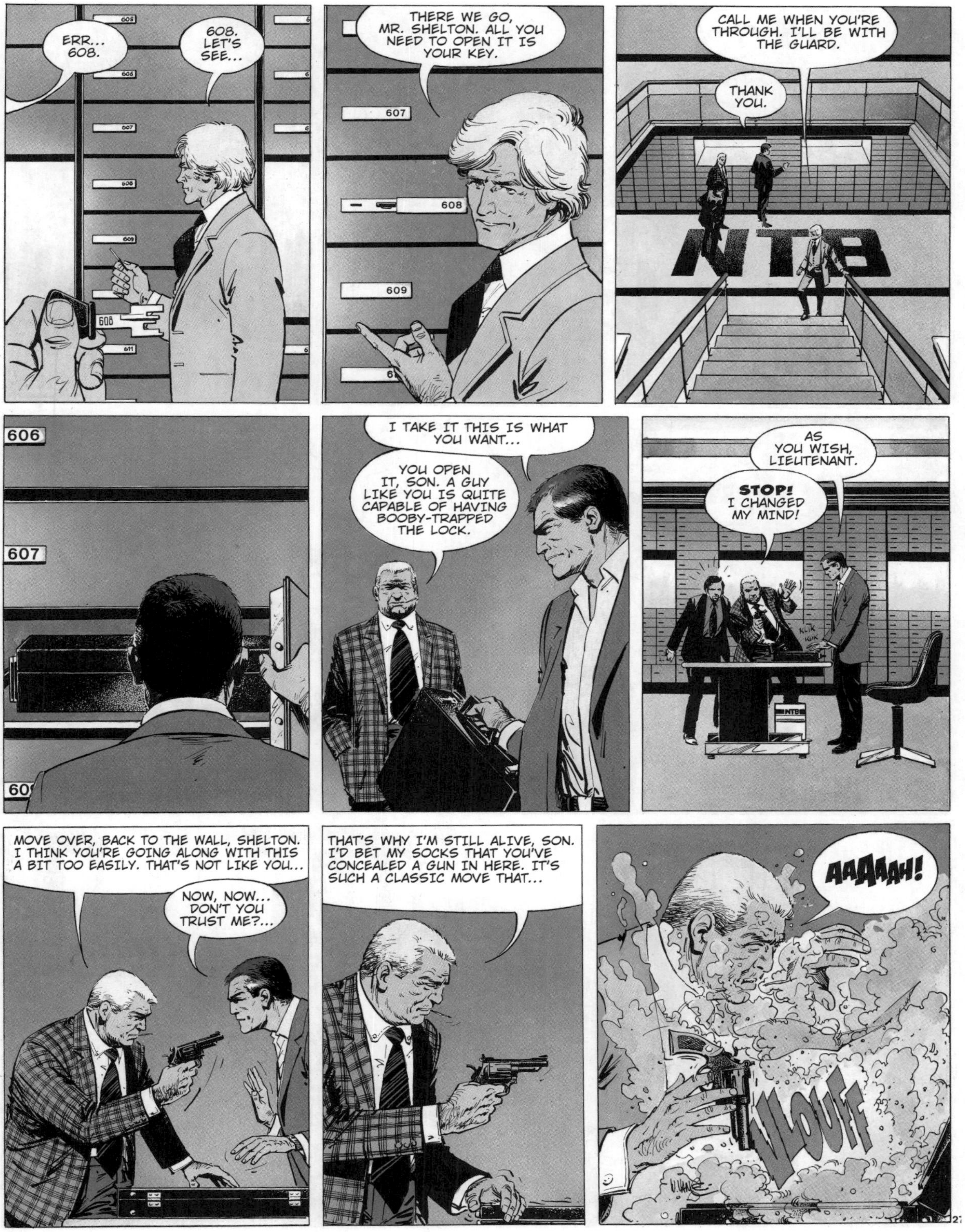

ERR... 608.
608. LET'S SEE...
THERE WE GO, MR. SHELTON. ALL YOU NEED TO OPEN IT IS YOUR KEY.
CALL ME WHEN YOU'RE THROUGH. I'LL BE WITH THE GUARD.
THANK YOU.
NTB
606
607
I TAKE IT THIS IS WHAT YOU WANT...
YOU OPEN IT, SON. A GUY LIKE YOU IS QUITE CAPABLE OF HAVING BOOBY-TRAPPED THE LOCK.
AS YOU WISH, LIEUTENANT.
STOP! I CHANGED MY MIND!
MOVE OVER, BACK TO THE WALL, SHELTON. I THINK YOU'RE GOING ALONG WITH THIS A BIT TOO EASILY. THAT'S NOT LIKE YOU...
NOW, NOW... DON'T YOU TRUST ME?...
THAT'S WHY I'M STILL ALIVE, SON. I'D BET MY SOCKS THAT YOU'VE CONCEALED A GUN IN HERE. IT'S SUCH A CLASSIC MOVE THAT...
AAAAAH!
VLOUFF

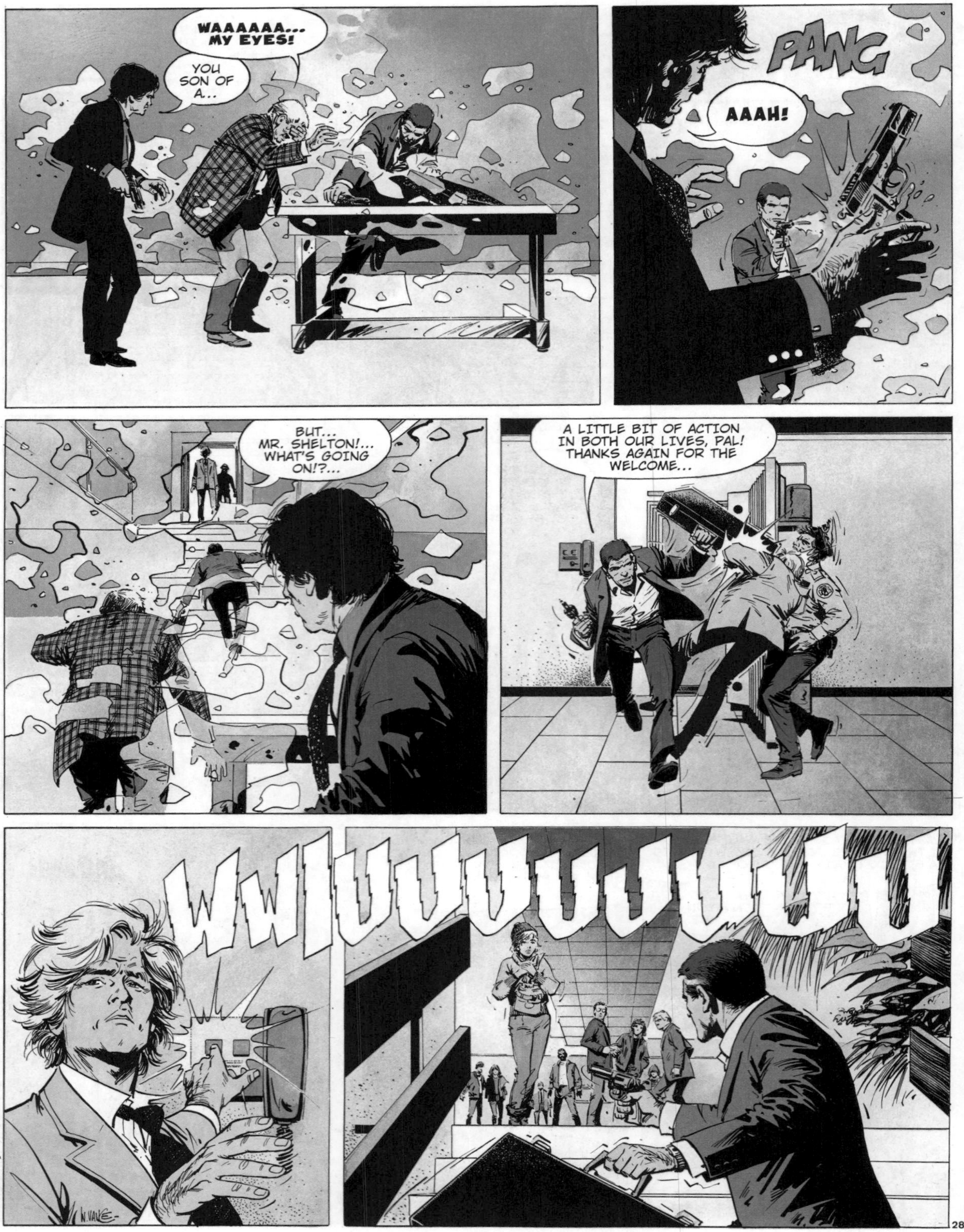
WAAAAAA... MY EYES!
YOU SON OF A...
PANG
AAAH!
BUT... MR. SHELTON!... WHAT'S GOING ON!?...
A LITTLE BIT OF ACTION IN BOTH OUR LIVES, PAL! THANKS AGAIN FOR THE WELCOME...
WWIUUUUUUUUU
W. VANCE
28

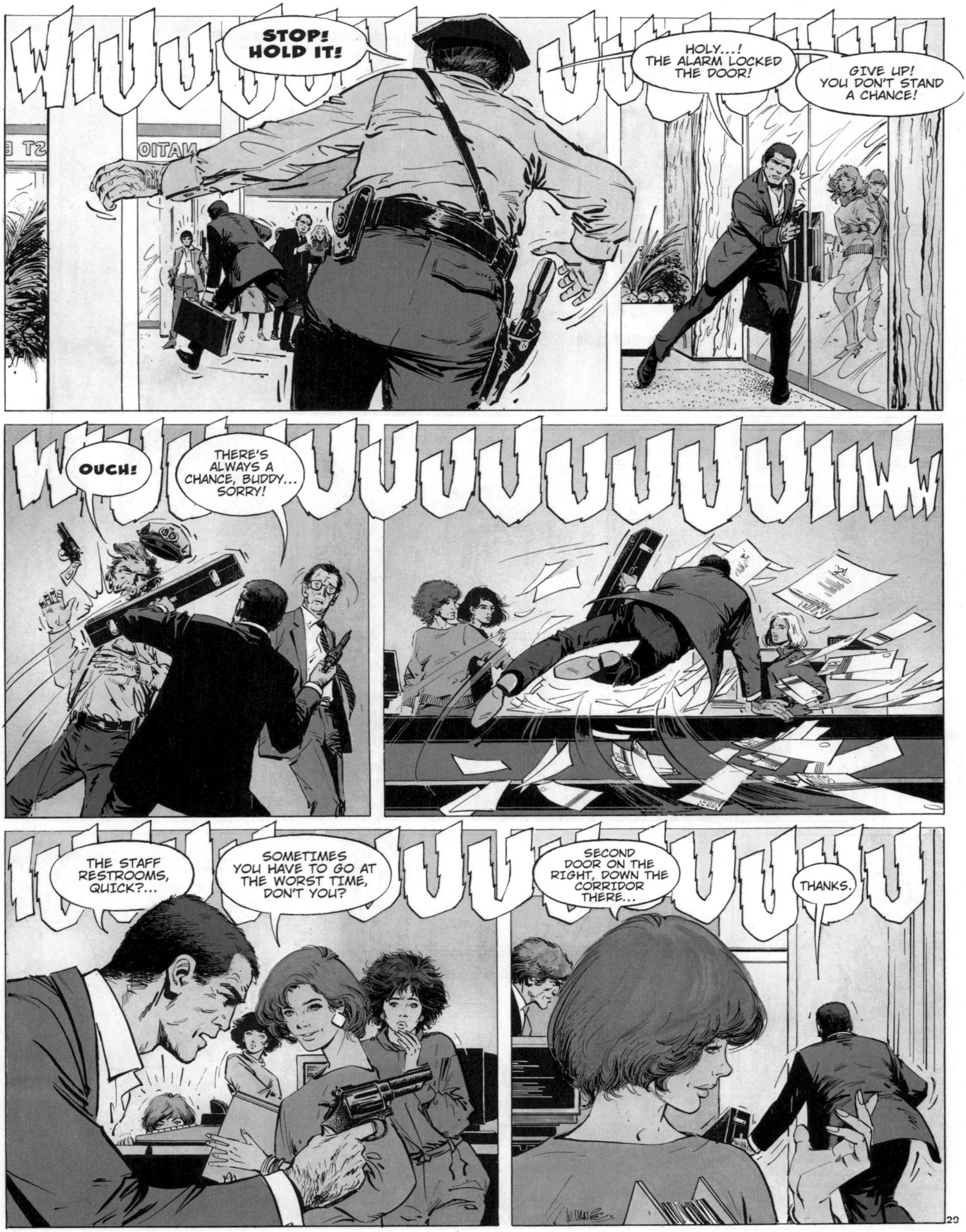
STOP! HOLD IT!
HOLY...! THE ALARM LOCKED THE DOOR!
GIVE UP! YOU DON'T STAND A CHANCE!
OUCH!
THERE'S ALWAYS A CHANCE, BUDDY... SORRY!
THE STAFF RESTROOMS, QUICK?...
SOMETIMES YOU HAVE TO GO AT THE WORST TIME, DON'T YOU?
SECOND DOOR ON THE RIGHT, DOWN THE CORRIDOR THERE...
THANKS.

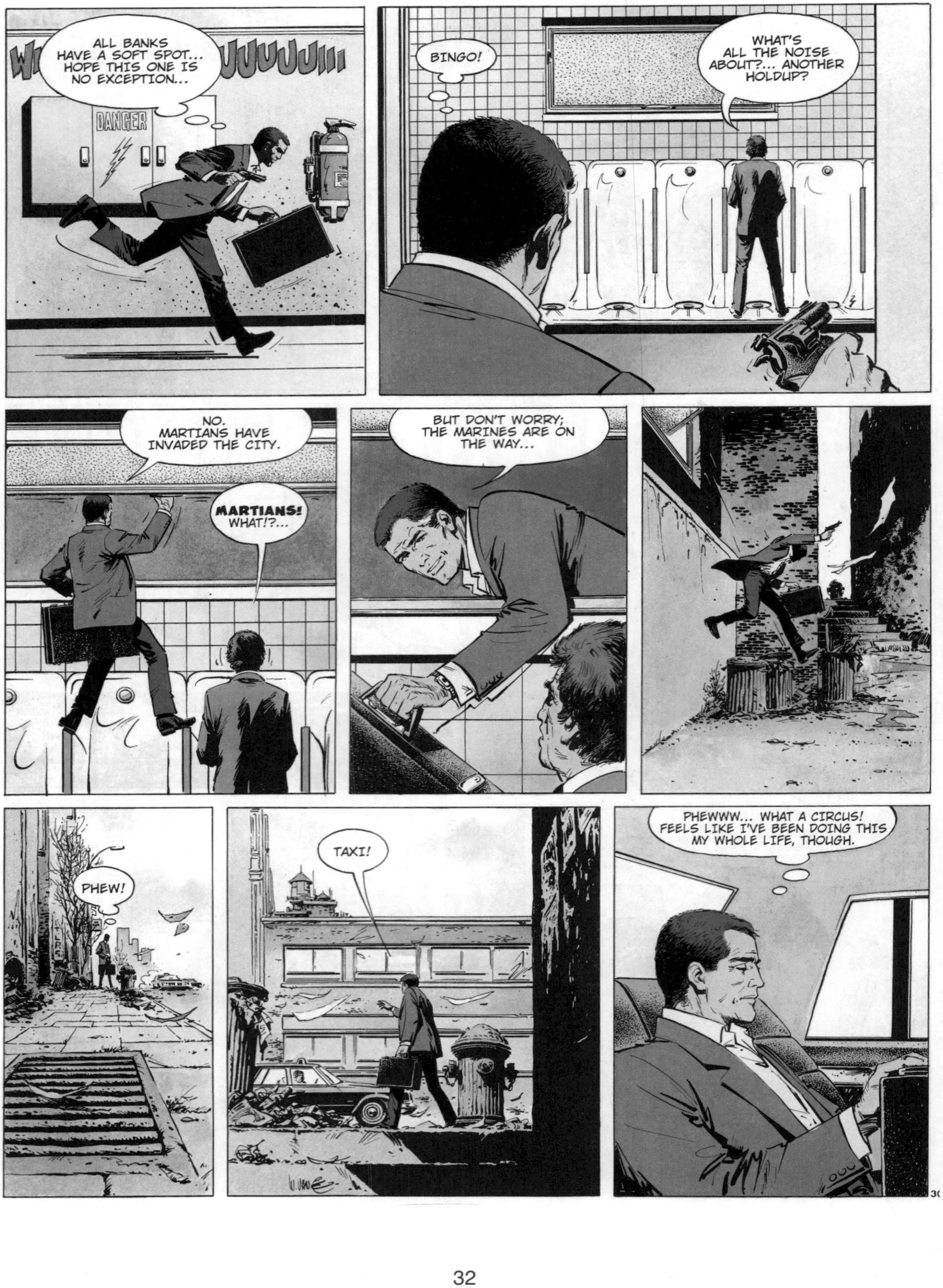

ALL BANKS HAVE A SOFT SPOT... HOPE THIS ONE IS NO EXCEPTION...
BINGO!
WHAT'S ALL THE NOISE ABOUT?... ANOTHER HOLDUP?
NO. MARTIANS HAVE INVADED THE CITY.
MARTIANS! WHAT!?...
BUT DON'T WORRY; THE MARINES ARE ON THE WAY...
PHEW!
TAXI!
PHEWWW... WHAT A CIRCUS! FEELS LIKE I'VE BEEN DOING THIS MY WHOLE LIFE, THOUGH.

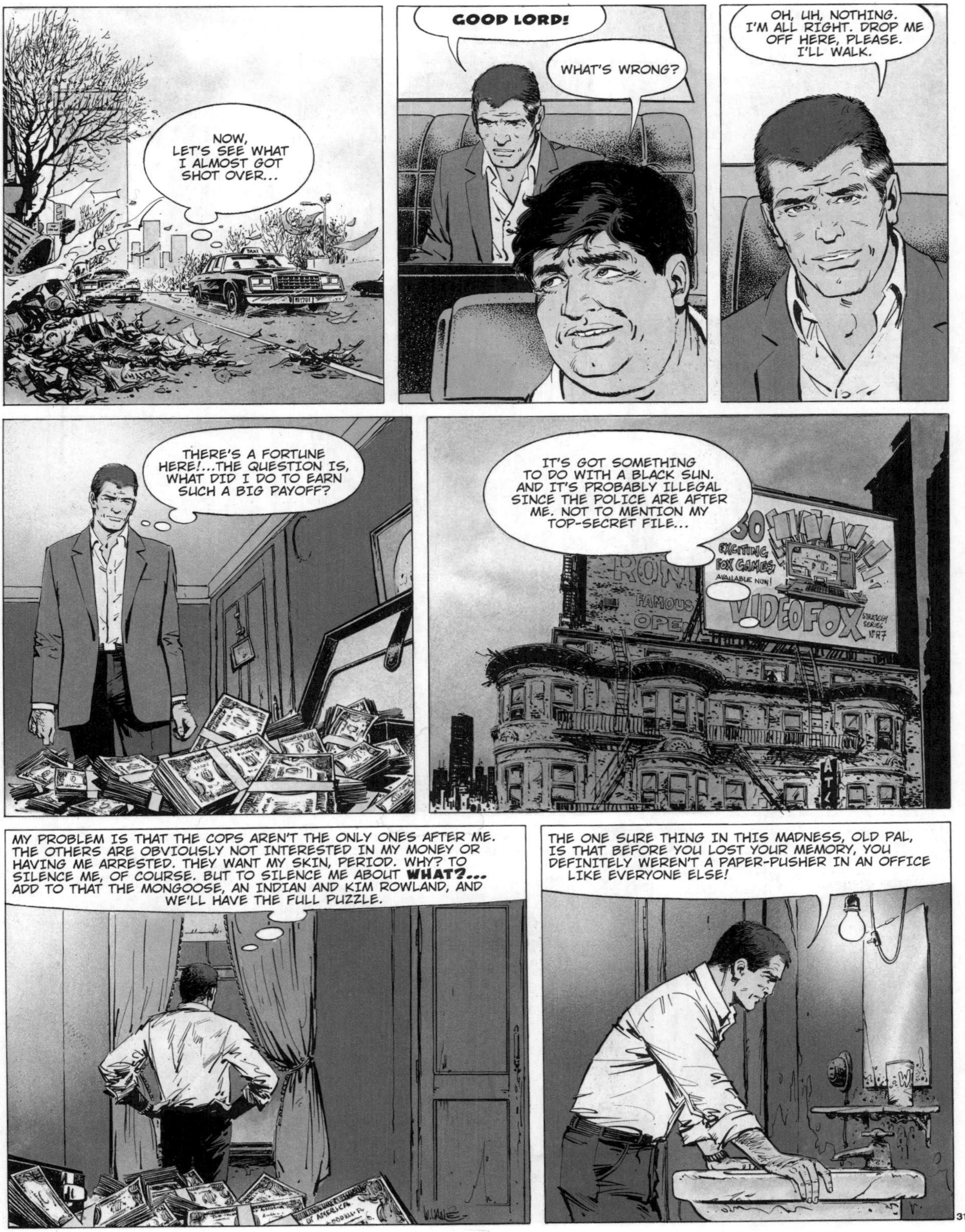
NOW, LET'S SEE WHAT I ALMOST GOT SHOT OVER...
GOOD LORD!
WHAT'S WRONG?
OH, UH, NOTHING. I'M ALL RIGHT. DROP ME OFF HERE, PLEASE. I'LL WALK.
THERE'S A FORTUNE HERE!...THE QUESTION IS, WHAT DID I DO TO EARN SUCH A BIG PAYOFF?
IT'S GOT SOMETHING TO DO WITH A BLACK SUN. AND IT'S PROBABLY ILLEGAL SINCE THE POLICE ARE AFTER ME. NOT TO MENTION MY TOP-SECRET FILE...
30 EXCITING FOX GAMES AVAILABLE NOW!
VIDEOFOX
STRATEGY SERIES Nº7
MY PROBLEM IS THAT THE COPS AREN'T THE ONLY ONES AFTER ME. THE OTHERS ARE OBVIOUSLY NOT INTERESTED IN MY MONEY OR HAVING ME ARRESTED. THEY WANT MY SKIN, PERIOD. WHY? TO SILENCE ME, OF COURSE. BUT TO SILENCE ME ABOUT **WHAT?...** ADD TO THAT THE MONGOOSE, AN INDIAN AND KIM ROWLAND, AND WE'LL HAVE THE FULL PUZZLE.
THE ONE SURE THING IN THIS MADNESS, OLD PAL, IS THAT BEFORE YOU LOST YOUR MEMORY, YOU DEFINITELY WEREN'T A PAPER-PUSHER IN AN OFFICE LIKE EVERYONE ELSE!
31

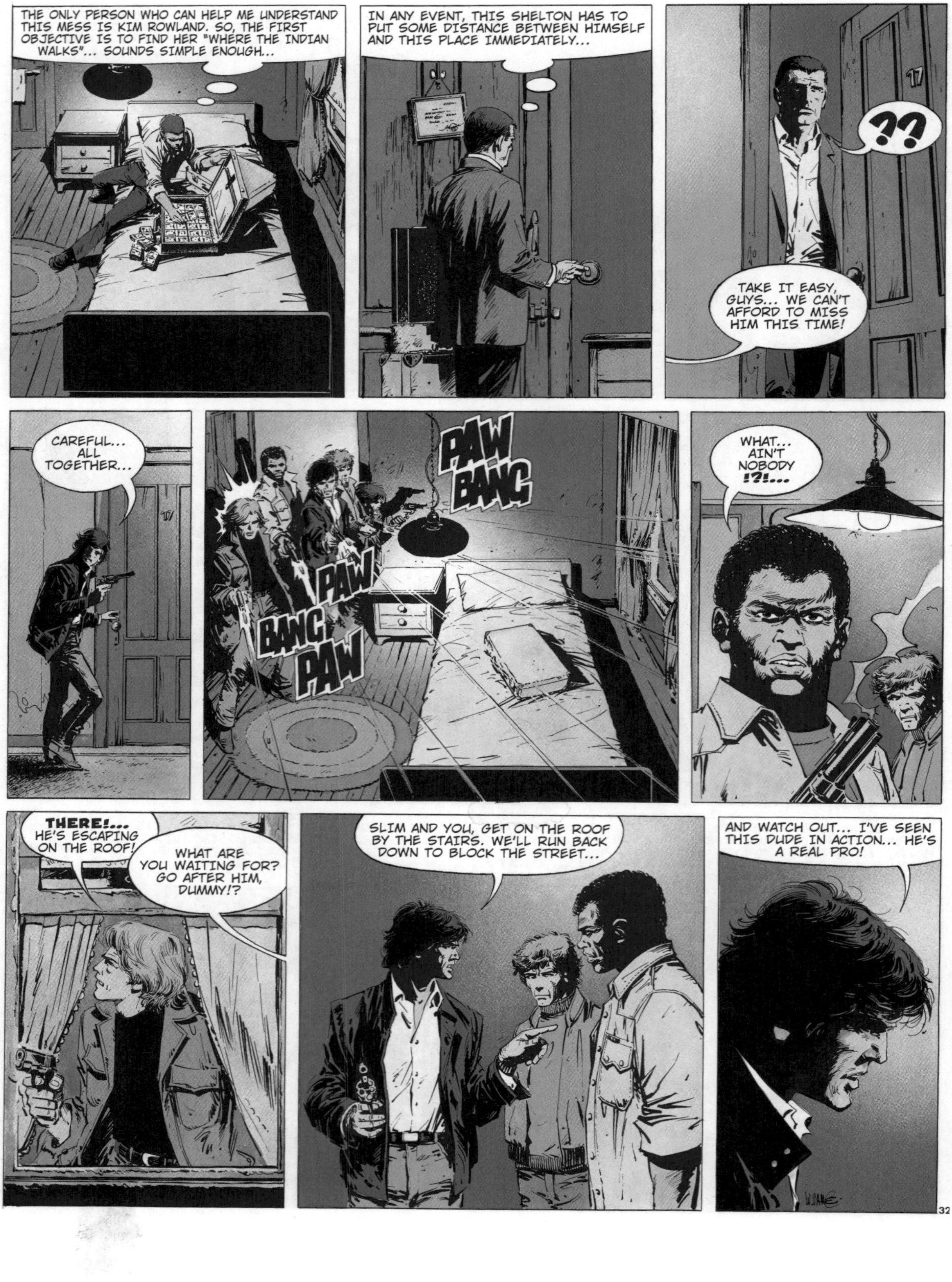
THE ONLY PERSON WHO CAN HELP ME UNDERSTAND THIS MESS IS KIM ROWLAND. SO, THE FIRST OBJECTIVE IS TO FIND HER "WHERE THE INDIAN WALKS"... SOUNDS SIMPLE ENOUGH...
IN ANY EVENT, THIS SHELTON HAS TO PUT SOME DISTANCE BETWEEN HIMSELF AND THIS PLACE IMMEDIATELY...
??
TAKE IT EASY, GUYS... WE CAN'T AFFORD TO MISS HIM THIS TIME!
CAREFUL... ALL TOGETHER...
PAW
BANG
PAW
BANG
PAW
WHAT... AIN'T NOBODY !?!...
THERE!... HE'S ESCAPING ON THE ROOF!
WHAT ARE YOU WAITING FOR? GO AFTER HIM, DUMMY!?
SLIM AND YOU, GET ON THE ROOF BY THE STAIRS. WE'LL RUN BACK DOWN TO BLOCK THE STREET...
AND WATCH OUT... I'VE SEEN THIS DUDE IN ACTION... HE'S A REAL PRO!
32

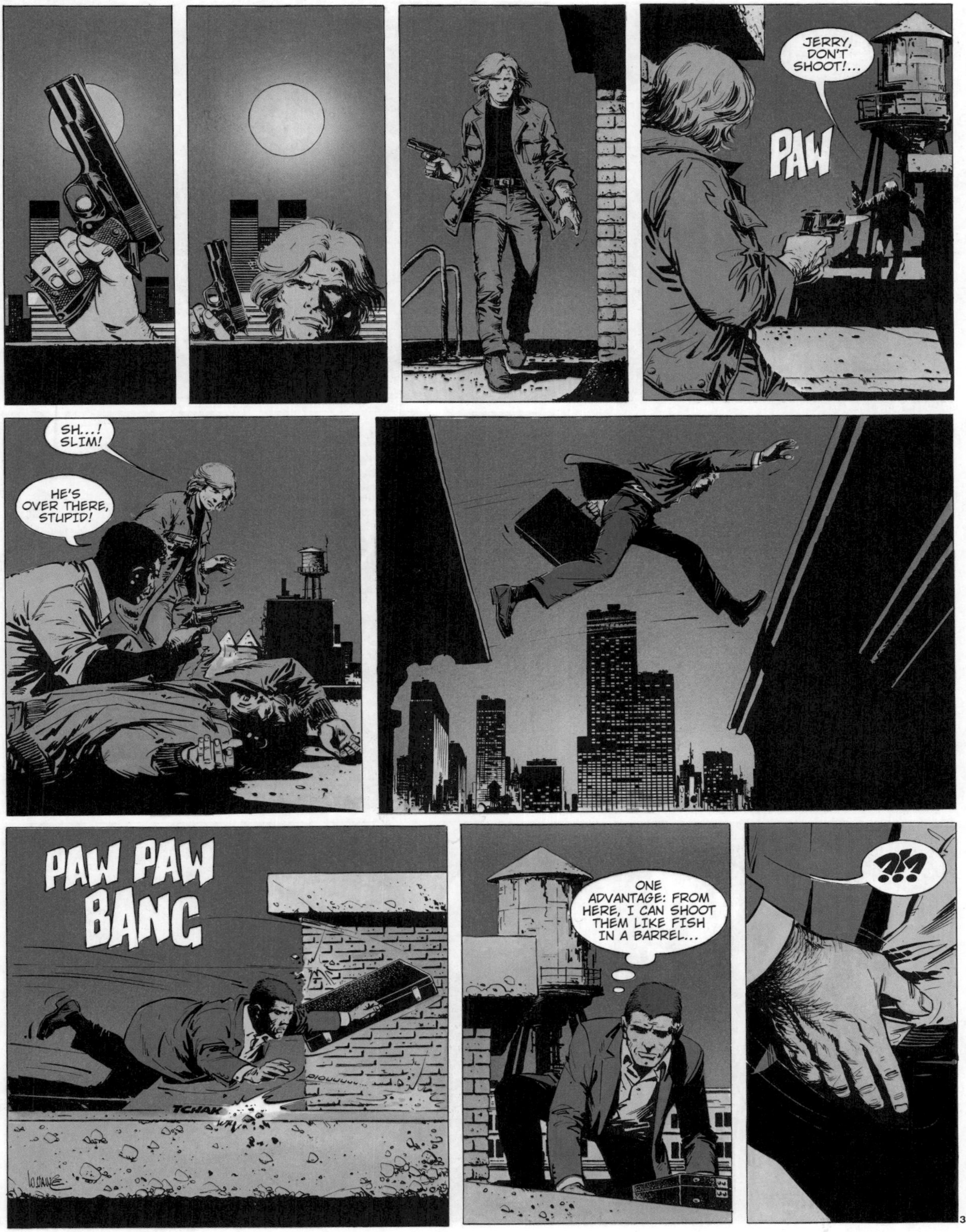

JERRY, DON'T SHOOT!...
PAW
SH...! SLIM!
HE'S OVER THERE, STUPID!
PAW PAW
BANG
TCHAK
ONE ADVANTAGE: FROM HERE, I CAN SHOOT THEM LIKE FISH IN A BARREL...
?!?

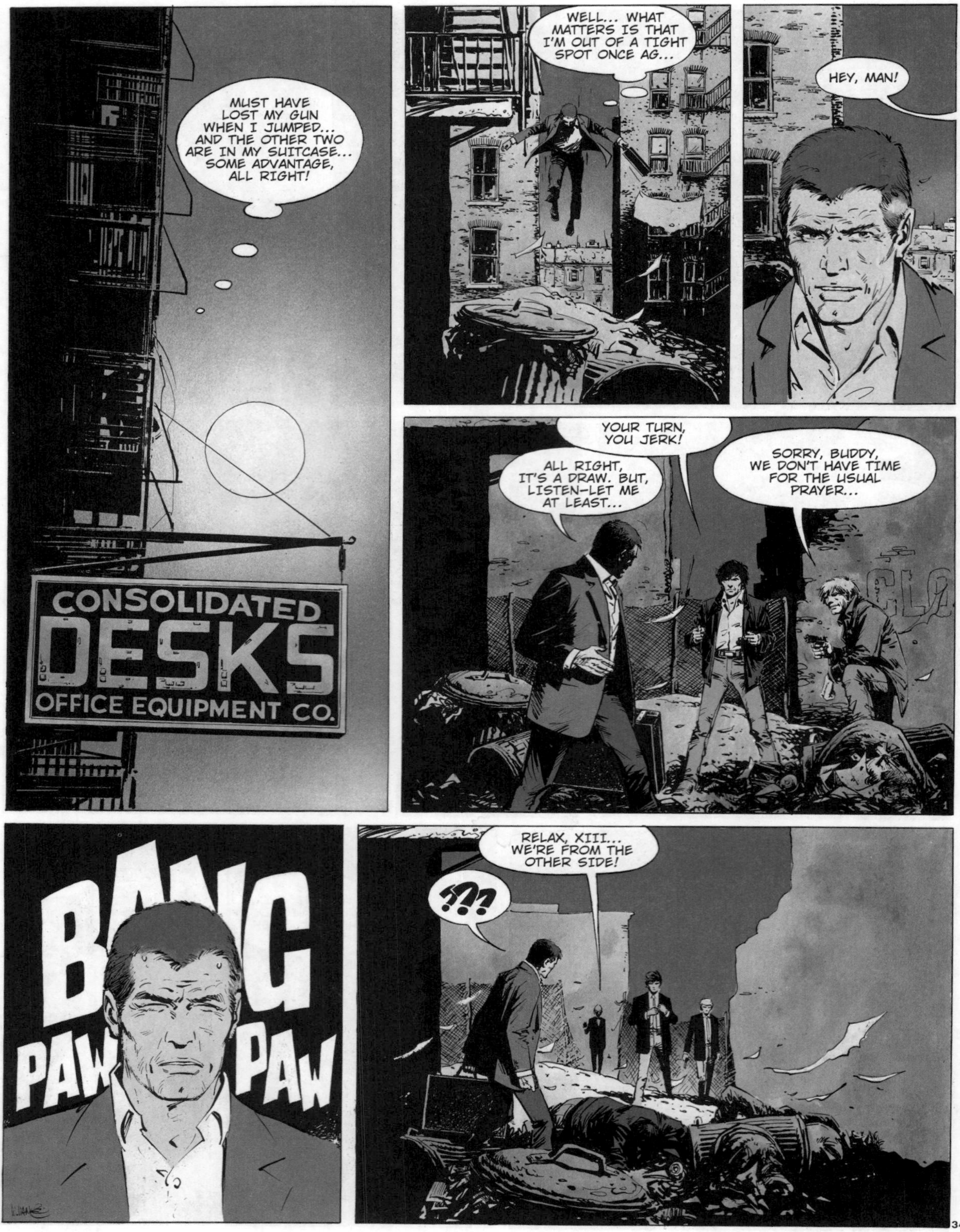

MUST HAVE LOST MY GUN WHEN I JUMPED... AND THE OTHER TWO ARE IN MY SUITCASE... SOME ADVANTAGE, ALL RIGHT!
CONSOLIDATED DESKS OFFICE EQUIPMENT CO.
WELL... WHAT MATTERS IS THAT I'M OUT OF A TIGHT SPOT ONCE AG...
HEY, MAN!
YOUR TURN, YOU JERK!
ALL RIGHT, IT'S A DRAW. BUT, LISTEN–LET ME AT LEAST...
SORRY, BUDDY, WE DON'T HAVE TIME FOR THE USUAL PRAYER...
BANG
PAW PAW
RELAX, XIII... WE'RE FROM THE OTHER SIDE!
???
34

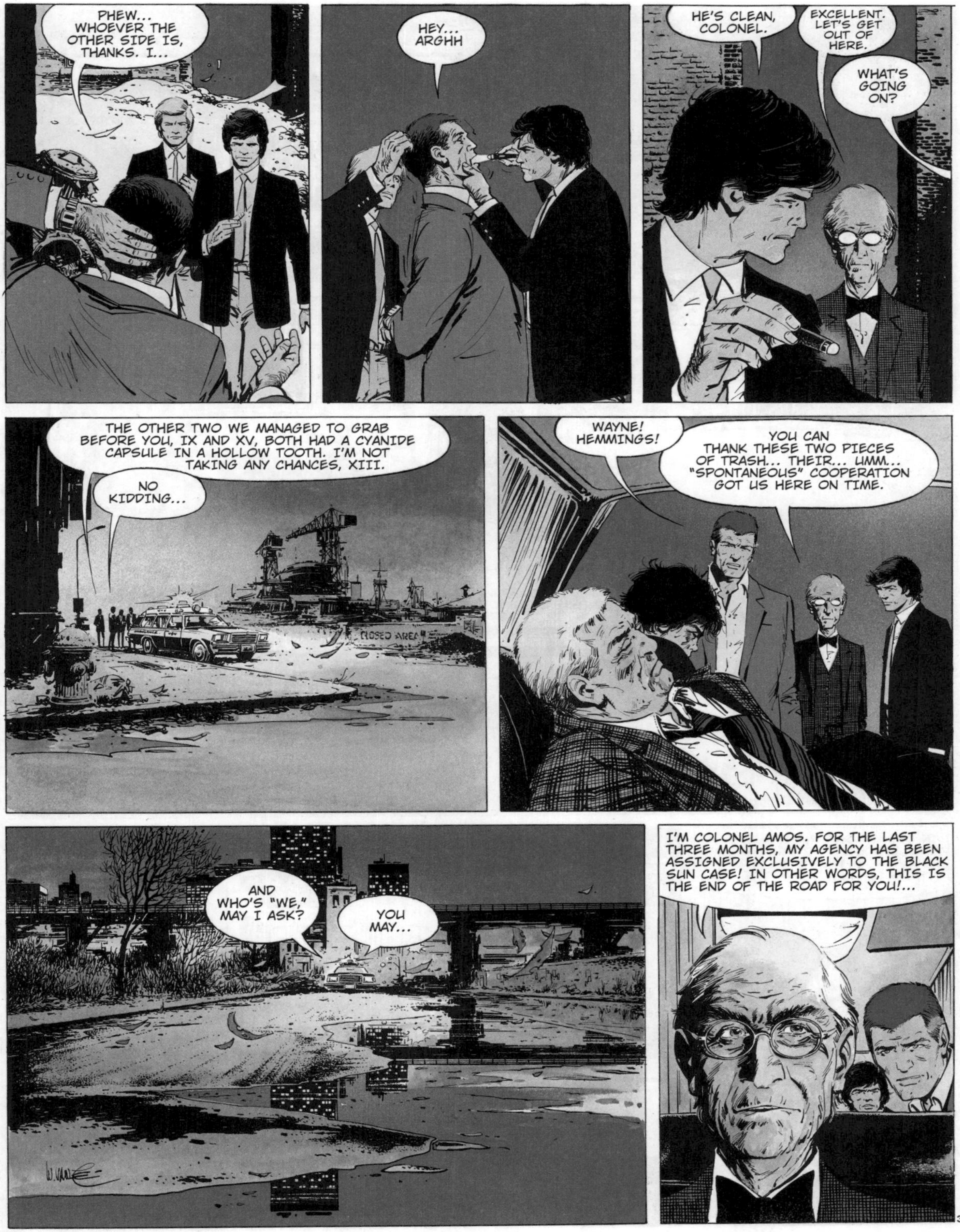
PHEW... WHOEVER THE OTHER SIDE IS, THANKS. I...
HEY... ARGHH
HE'S CLEAN, COLONEL.
EXCELLENT. LET'S GET OUT OF HERE.
WHAT'S GOING ON?
THE OTHER TWO WE MANAGED TO GRAB BEFORE YOU, IX AND XV, BOTH HAD A CYANIDE CAPSULE IN A HOLLOW TOOTH. I'M NOT TAKING ANY CHANCES, XIII.
NO KIDDING...
CLOSED AREA
WAYNE! HEMMINGS!
YOU CAN THANK THESE TWO PIECES OF TRASH... THEIR... UMM... "SPONTANEOUS" COOPERATION GOT US HERE ON TIME.
AND WHO'S "WE," MAY I ASK?
YOU MAY...
I'M COLONEL AMOS. FOR THE LAST THREE MONTHS, MY AGENCY HAS BEEN ASSIGNED EXCLUSIVELY TO THE BLACK SUN CASE! IN OTHER WORDS, THIS IS THE END OF THE ROAD FOR YOU!...
35

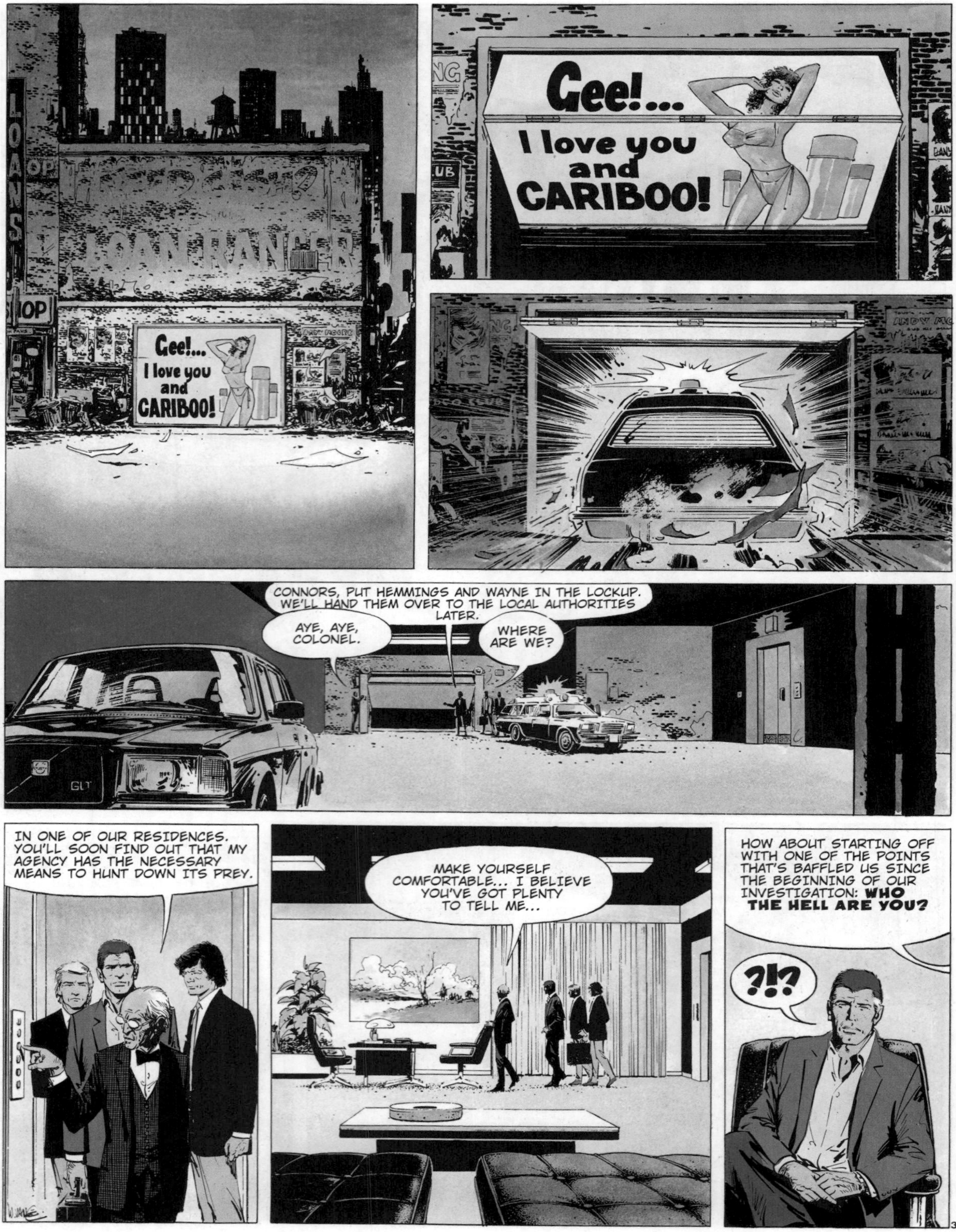
LOANS
SHOP
LOAN RANGER
Gee!... I love you and CARIBOO!
Gee!... I love you and CARIBOO!
CONNORS, PUT HEMMINGS AND WAYNE IN THE LOCKUP. WE'LL HAND THEM OVER TO THE LOCAL AUTHORITIES LATER.
AYE, AYE, COLONEL.
WHERE ARE WE?
IN ONE OF OUR RESIDENCES. YOU'LL SOON FIND OUT THAT MY AGENCY HAS THE NECESSARY MEANS TO HUNT DOWN ITS PREY.
MAKE YOURSELF COMFORTABLE... I BELIEVE YOU'VE GOT PLENTY TO TELL ME...
HOW ABOUT STARTING OFF WITH ONE OF THE POINTS THAT'S BAFFLED US SINCE THE BEGINNING OF OUR INVESTIGATION: **WHO THE HELL ARE YOU?**
?!?
36

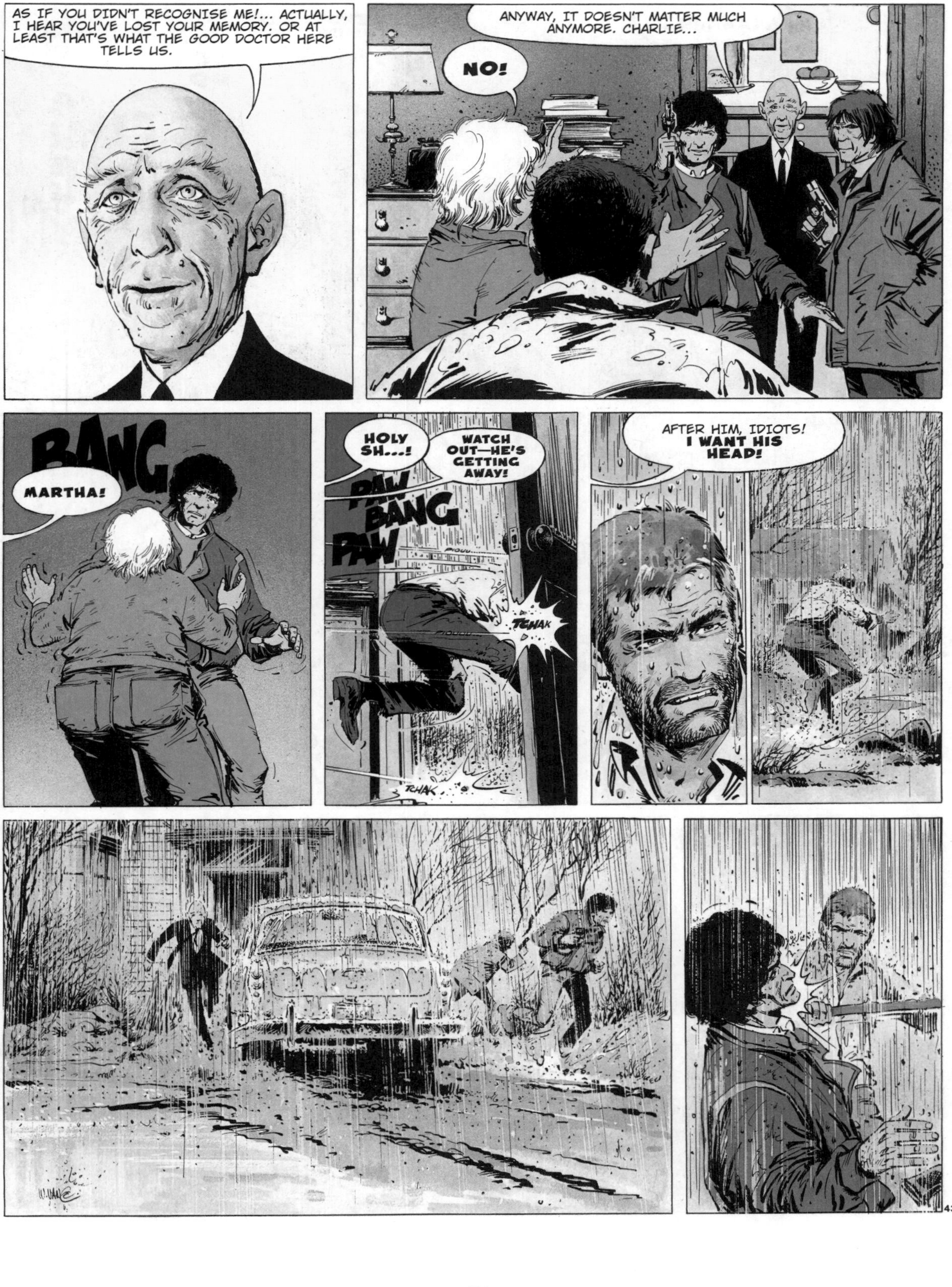
AS IF YOU DIDN'T RECOGNISE ME!... ACTUALLY, I HEAR YOU'VE LOST YOUR MEMORY. OR AT LEAST THAT'S WHAT THE GOOD DOCTOR HERE TELLS US.
ANYWAY, IT DOESN'T MATTER MUCH ANYMORE. CHARLIE...
NO!
BANG
MARTHA!
HOLY SH...!
WATCH OUT—HE'S GETTING AWAY!
PAW BANG PAW
TCHAK
TCHAK
AFTER HIM, IDIOTS! I WANT HIS HEAD!
43

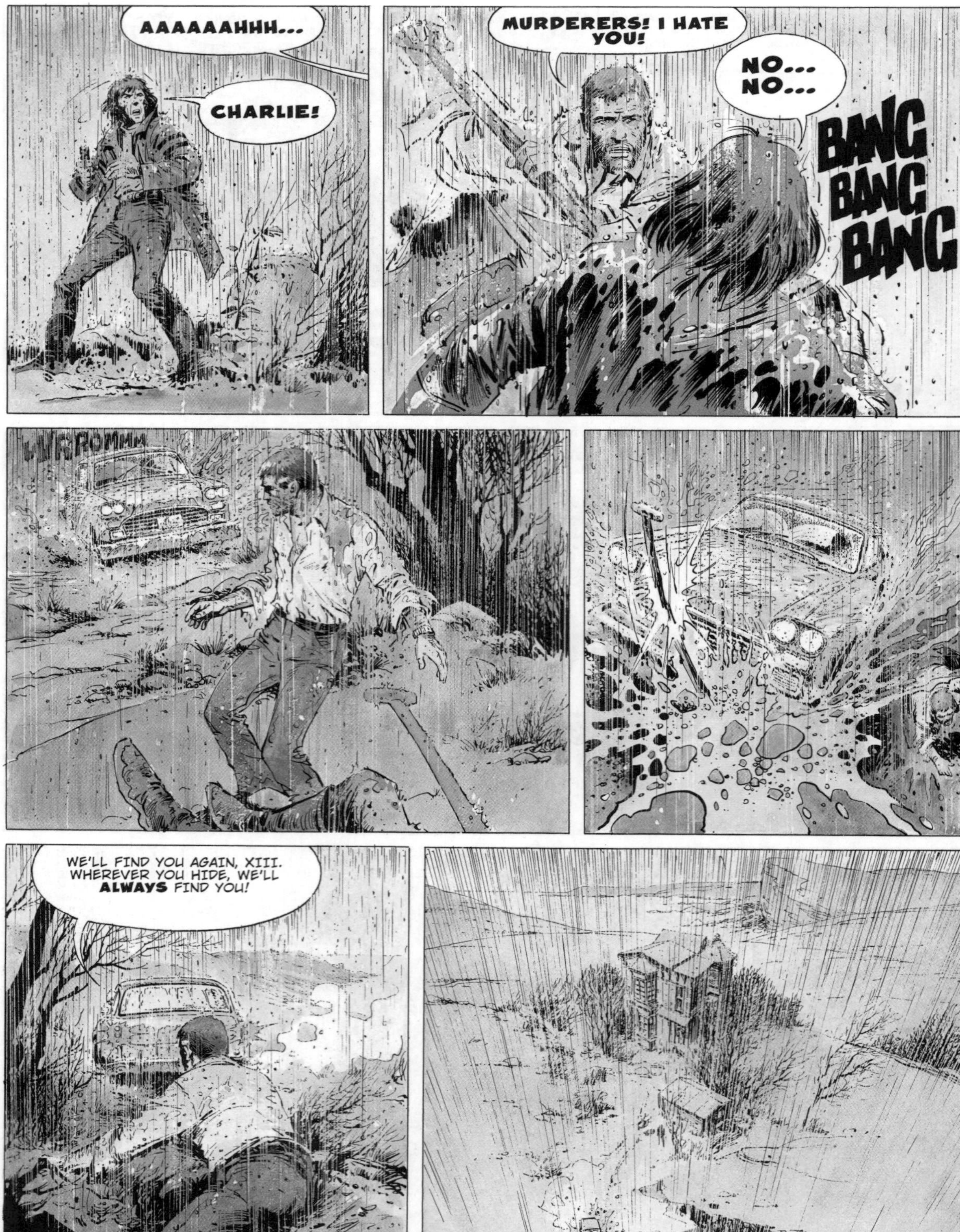
AAAAAAHHH...
CHARLIE!
MURDERERS! I HATE YOU!
NO... NO...
BANG BANG BANG
WRROMMM
WE'LL FIND YOU AGAIN, XIII. WHEREVER YOU HIDE, WE'LL **ALWAYS** FIND YOU!
44

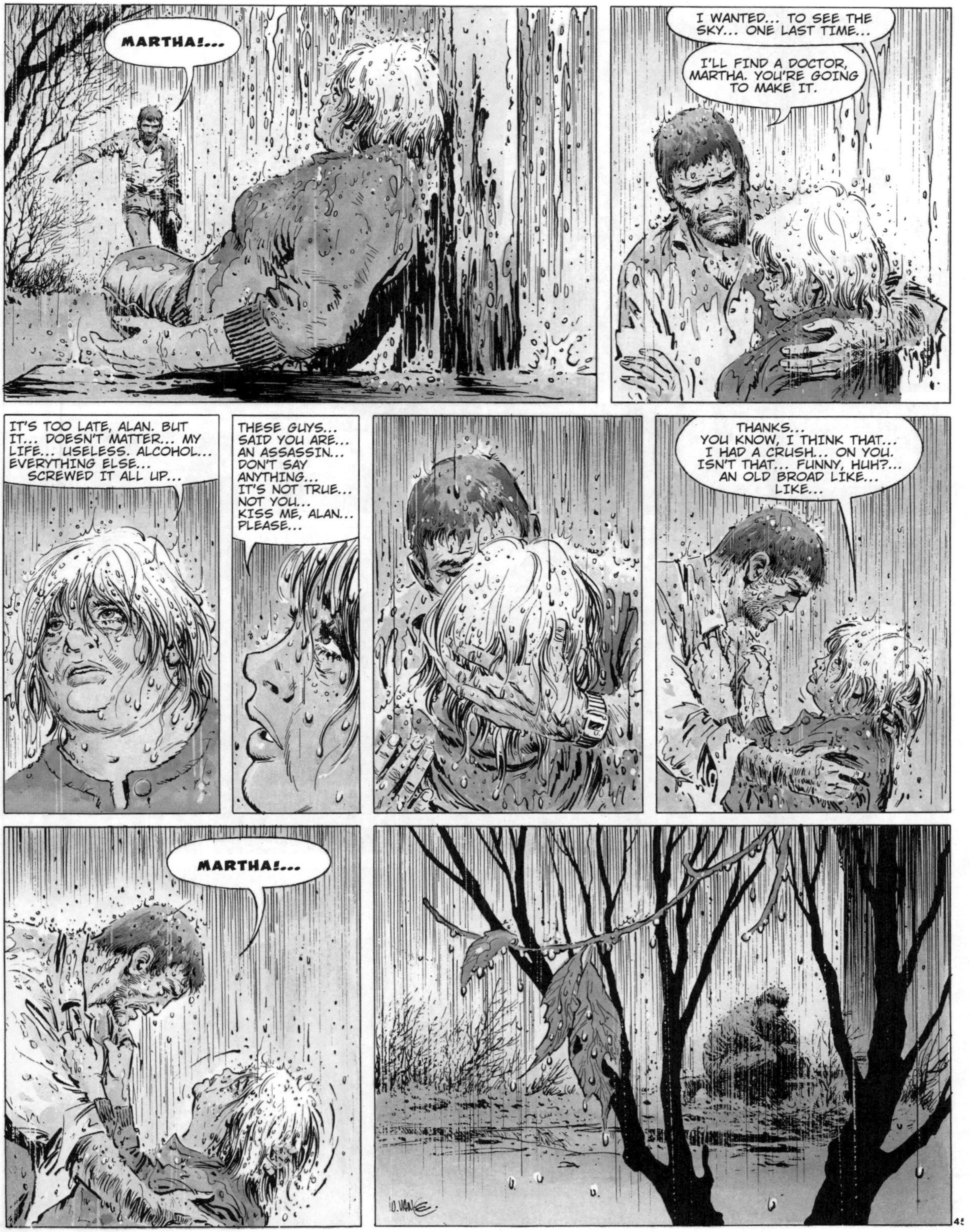
MARTHA!...
I WANTED... TO SEE THE SKY... ONE LAST TIME...
I'LL FIND A DOCTOR, MARTHA. YOU'RE GOING TO MAKE IT.
IT'S TOO LATE, ALAN. BUT IT... DOESN'T MATTER... MY LIFE... USELESS. ALCOHOL... EVERYTHING ELSE... SCREWED IT ALL UP...
THESE GUYS... SAID YOU ARE... AN ASSASSIN... DON'T SAY ANYTHING... IT'S NOT TRUE... NOT YOU... KISS ME, ALAN... PLEASE...
THANKS... YOU KNOW, I THINK THAT... I HAD A CRUSH... ON YOU. ISN'T THAT... FUNNY, HUH?... AN OLD BROAD LIKE... LIKE...
MARTHA!...
W. VANCE
45

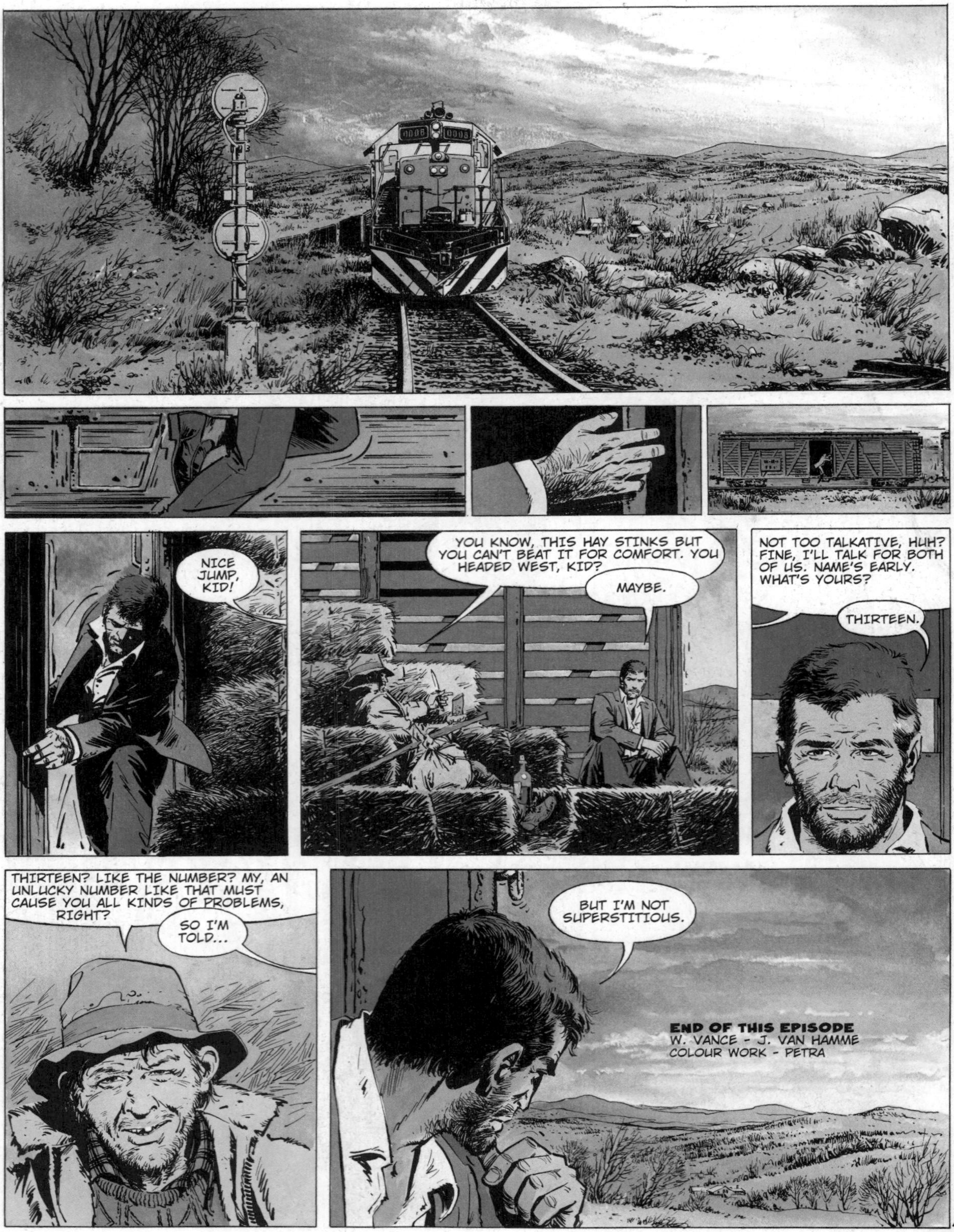
NICE JUMP, KID!
YOU KNOW, THIS HAY STINKS BUT YOU CAN'T BEAT IT FOR COMFORT. YOU HEADED WEST, KID?
MAYBE.
NOT TOO TALKATIVE, HUH? FINE, I'LL TALK FOR BOTH OF US. NAME'S EARLY. WHAT'S YOURS?
THIRTEEN.
THIRTEEN? LIKE THE NUMBER? MY, AN UNLUCKY NUMBER LIKE THAT MUST CAUSE YOU ALL KINDS OF PROBLEMS, RIGHT?
SO I'M TOLD...
BUT I'M NOT SUPERSTITIOUS.
END OF THIS EPISODE
W. VANCE - J. VAN HAMME
COLOUR WORK - PETRA
46